Bone Fires

Bone Fires

New and Selected Poems

MARK JARMAN

SARABANDE  BOOKS
LOUISVILLE, KENTUCKY

Managing Editor
Sarabande Books, Inc.
2234 Dundee Road, Suite 200
Louisville, KY 40205

Library of Congress Cataloging-in-Publication Data

Jarman, Mark.
  Bone fires : new and selected poems / by Mark Jarman.
    p. cm.
  ISBN 978-1-932511-89-5 (pbk. : alk. paper) — ISBN 978-1-932511-92-5
  (hardcover : alk. paper)
  I. Title.
  PS3560.A537B66 2011
  811'.54—dc22

                                        2010024678

Cover Art by Donald Jarman.

Cover and interior text design by Kirkby Gann Tittle.

Manufactured in Canada.

This book is printed on acid-free paper.

Sarabande Books is a nonprofit literary organization.

This project is supported in part by an award from the National Endowment for the Arts.

The Kentucky Arts Council, the state arts agency, supports Sarabande Books with state tax dollars and federal funding from the National Endowment for the Arts.

For Amy

"And I believed her."

Contents

Questions for Ecclesiastes (1997)

Unholy Sonnets (2000)

To the Green Man (2004)

Epistles (2007)

Acknowledgements

"Snoring," "Black Phoebe," "Devereux Lagoon," "Dispatch from Devereux Slough," "From the Garden Toad," "Marine Layer," "Overcast on Ellwood Mesa," "September Song," "Shorebreak," "Sundowner," "Surgeons," "The Crystal Ship," "To a Dead Sea Lion at Sands Beach," *American Poetry Review*; "Bone Fires," *The Atlantic Monthly*; "Your Neighbor as Yourself," *Cumberland Poetry Review*; "The Prayer Chain," "Heaven," *Five Points*; "Monday," *Georgia Review*; "Encounter," *The Hudson Review*; "Time Machine," *The New Criterion*; "Good God," *New Ohio Review*; "The Wee Spider," "Last Walk at Home," *Northwest Review*; "R. S. Thomas," *The New Republic*; "Haiku," *Ploughshares*; "Interesting Times," *Poetry*; "Mary Smart," *Shenandoah*; "In the Rose Garden," *Slate*; "Family Fugue," *Terminus*; "Ending with a Line by Curtis Mayfield," *Yale Review*.

"How My Sister, My Mother, and I Still Travel Down Balwearie Road," Sutton Hoo Press, Broadside, 1991.

"To a Brainy Child in Distress," *Hurricane Blues: Poems About Katrina and Rita*, Southeast Missouri State University Press, 2006.

North Sea, Cleveland State Poetry Center, 1978; *The Rote Walker*, Carnegie-Mellon University Press, 1981; *Far and Away*, Carnegie-Mellon University Press, 1985; *The Black Riviera*, Wesleyan University Press, 1990; *Questions for Ecclesiastes*, Story Line Press, 1997; *Unholy Sonnets*, Story Line Press, 2000; *To the Green Man*, Sarabande Books, 2004; *Epistles*, Sarabande Books, 2007.

Poems from *Questions for Ecclesiastes* and *To the Green Man* are dedicated as follows: "Unholy Sonnet 18" is for Roy Gottfried; "Transfiguration" is for Michelle Boisseau; "Questions for Ecclesiastes" is for Judson Mitcham; "Last Suppers" is for Andrew Hudgins; "To the Green Man" is for Philip Wilby; "The Excitement" is for Wyatt Prunty; "The Secret Ocean" is for Claire and Zoë; "Summer" is for Amy.

My profound thanks to friends who read this manuscript and offered suggestions—Michelle Boisseau, Christopher Buckley, Garrett Hongo, Judson Mitcham, Terri Witek, and especially Dick Allen. Thanks, too, to Vanderbilt University for giving me time to put the manuscript together.

Please note: ∞ stands for a stanza break when one is lost in pagination.

Bone Fires

How My Sister, My Mother, and I Still Travel Down Balwearie Road

In a night where ice and darkness have made a pact, the road appears.

It has found its way under trees whose branches, carved from anthracite,

Smudge out the stars. Voices are approaching, though it is hardly possible,

Unless the cold-killed night speaks from the grave. There is laughter

And a grinding swish of friction. This is far, far north, where the dead night keeps

Its compacts with darkness, with cold, with trees and stars that agree to die.

Yet down the road come voices and a sound of shoes sliding on ice.

Through the darkness come a boy and girl, and a woman, in scarves and cloth coats.

They have broken the boundaries of time and slide out of the night, laughing,

Then wait where the road ends for the bus, two tiers of light and warmth, which comes to take them home.

It is still cold, still dark, just as I said, and late. But not as late as I thought.

New Poems

The Wee Spider

No moment is ever isolated
With history elsewhere, drilling its stitches.
We arrived at Glasgow, the mouth of the Clyde,
Through autumn gales, and a steward's death.
"How young they start them," my mother wrote
About our steward, not the drowned boy
(We assumed he was a boy, as the ship turned
In the storm, bucking the waves to find nobody).
The world works and works its machines,
But most lives make it and memory breeds
Its combs and catacombs, part by part.
A huddle of us was piped ashore, the ship
Was a black and white berg on green ice-water,
And a piper in his kilt skirled on the launch.
Then, a man in camel hair hunter's costume
Opened his case and put his pipes together,
And asked him, "D'ye ken 'The Wee Spider'?"
The two played together as the dockside roofs,
Wet slate like coal, shifted and shone,
And their music went reeling across to shore
And a pastor's family from California
Began its sojourn. Mid-century Scotland.

Ah, the twentieth century, the last century now,

Yet still attached, still holding on.

Years later, when I returned to our town—

A failing linoleum factory capital

That looked across the firth at the real capital

As if it were purgatory gazing at paradise—

And attended the small dying church my father served,

With the old who were old when I was a child,

I was told the reason it was dying. "Your father left,"

Said a stout man who had been a slim teenager,

A boy who babysat me one night

And brought me water in a china tea cup.

Against the large events of the time, the great shifting

And shining of leaders and nations, this small remembrance,

"Your father left," from a roughneck on a North Sea oil rig.

Family Fugue

When Pup Dog drank he threw the cap away.

"I'm not your typical granddad," Pup Dog said,

"Cracking walnuts under the money tree.

If I come back, I'll come back as a jackass."

And Nora, his wife, my grandmother, responded,

"Oh dear, God wouldn't do the same thing to you twice."

When Pup Dog drank he threw the cap away.

Nora's ex-husband, Jim, spoke with his hands,

Planting his annuals in the air with their names

Or folding a frittata before your eyes.

His wife Ethelwyn explained him to his daughter

And smiled. "Out of sight, out of mind," she said.

Her son got everything and told my mother,

"The condo and its contents are all mine."

When Pup Dog drank he threw the cap away.

Grandmother Grace laughed and said Ethelwyn

Drove like the wind. On Sunday after church,

Ray, her husband, went to the opera.

"I can't take the responsibility!" he said, as she lay sick.

She let her grandchildren fiddle with her arm flesh.

Her teacups were like a collection of butterflies

Drenched in the cedar cupboard's preserving scent.

When Pup Dog drank he threw the cap away.

Grace, the first to die, laughed on the freeway

As Ethelwyn drove like the wind. That's what she said.

And Nora told her Pup Dog, he was a jackass

And God would never make him one again.

And Ray couldn't take the responsibility.

And Jim outlived them all, planting his flowers

Before your eyes, speaking with his hands.

When Pup Dog drank he threw the cap away.

They were all from some place else, then California.

They drove cars with power windows. They used swear words.

They slept in king-sized beds in separate rooms.

And drank Manhattans. And called my parents "the kids."

They looked old when they were middle-aged.

And in pictures from their youth, they look like children.

Your Neighbor as Yourself

Laughing or crying, it's hard to tell from here,

The widow mows her lawn in a big straw hat,

Riding the mower her husband used to cruise on,

Mounted with his thermos of margaritas.

I could go over and help her rake the tears up,

That is, the cut grass, lying frail and swept

By semi-shadows of her gold sombrero.

But I can tell the shade of privacy

Covers her face with what now looks like pleasure.

So many of us want our solitude.

It could be *that* desire is our wildness,

Retained as predilection—to be alone,

Unhelped by caring neighbors or caregivers.

I've heard a dolphin expert say her creatures

Do not desire society with us,

Despite the frolicking around sea vessels.

They're wild with nothing human in their make-up.

They don't want to perform for our delight

And they are not inviting us to swim.

The loneliness of everything created,

The solitude it needs to be itself,

Looks back at us when we are looking on.

These bars of tree trunk shadow on the grass,

Austere and clean, are blending as the sun sets

With another sort of shadow altogether,

Which folds them in, erasing their distinction,

Until there is no way to call them shadows

Or to call the other anything but night.

Time Machine

When we arrive, the future will adore us

As being so much better than it expected.

We went to school with thugs and contagion.

We went to school with tidal waves and felons.

And we turned out OK. We're at the future!

Greeting each one of us with a wet kiss,

And up until this moment, we're . . . But wait a minute.

That smell of roses and that taste of wine,

They may be just the opposite when we get there.

Even though we're better than expected,

Simply because we've made it, let's be careful.

Let's be careful hurtling toward the future,

Arms thrown open to embrace its billboard smile.

It may be just a very cramped apartment

With only Jean-Luc Godard for atmosphere,

A weeping parent, a disappointed child,

Pink nipples of the past turned gray.

And that fleet mechanism underfoot

Speeding us into transcendental space

May not allow us to stop anywhere.

Haiku

Things that can turn to shrapnel:
Steel and stone. Crockery.
Wood. Glass. And bone.

Mary Smart

When my mistakes flash back and half blind me
Like the ocular migraines I've had since I was little,
Glaring brassy unmeshed gears circling
Before my sight for minutes and then fading,
I think of the last time I sat with Mary Smart,
A pillar of my father's church in Scotland,
Upright in her wing chair, nearly ninety, reminiscing
While North Sea wind rattled the window panes.
A widow more than a decade, still worried
About the last words passed between her and her husband,
She told me how she found peace despite remorse.
After his death, she'd gone on retreat with friends,
All widows, to the island of Iona,
And in bed the first night in that holy place,
She lay among the other women listening
To what she thought were bells or bell-like voices,
Ringing or singing somewhere on the island.
And with them her husband David's voice returned,
Asking her please to loosen the tight bed sheet.
And her own voice returned saying she didn't like
To undo what the nurse had done. Last words.
At that he'd slipped into his final sleep.

And sleepless then she heard the music come,

Reaching her on the wind, up from the beach,

Among her roommates. (Were they listening, too?)

But only she could hear her husband's voice

And her voice, back and forth, in the dim ringing.

So much we can't retrieve, so much unsay.

She lay among the widows on Iona,

In their dorm room, on retreat, listening.

And when she knew that what she heard ringing

Was not bells but the stirring of the shells,

The shingle covering the beach she'd seen that day,

Made all of shells, of curving sea shell bodies,

Their hard thin surfaces knocking in the wind,

All of them clinking, talking, talking, clinking,

A soothing wonder made her close her eyes.

It was not bells or voices that she heard,

And knowing what it was was like a pardon.

I think of Mary Smart, who was an old lady

When I was a wild wee boy, as she once called me.

She found a way to hear herself released

By the living world and remnants of the living.

She said, "Mark, you know we are not our bodies,"

And told me David would sit where I was sitting

And watch her wake up from her afternoon naps,

Then waver away, into her memory,

Less like a ghost, she said, than a figure of speech.

The Prayer Chain

Mother's on the telephone, forging a link
In the prayer chain, a tub of suds
And dishes steaming in the sun-white sink.
And I wonder if the twisted phone cord

Is part of it. But she explains
That someone in the church is ailing.
And she calls to start a chain
Of prayers. She tells me this with feeling.

A cloud has dimmed the kitchen. Her face
Hardens with conviction. Once the chain
Is forged the call will come back to our place,
The closing link, the praying done.

This is circa 1961,
Redondo Beach, South Bay Christian Church.
I wonder if there's still such a thing
To pull the suffering into the reach—

Of what? Those links in the prayer chain?
For wasn't it the casting of

A spell, the binding of a span
Of power? They would have called it Love,

Believers with this one sense of magic,
Stringing the gold of faith from voice
To voice. Like Rimbaud. Or like Blake,
Beholding the dread tyger in its throes.

But that's not what they thought, surely,
Or what she thought. And yet the chain
Reached from earth to heaven, really,
Like the chain Milton imagined,

Dangling planet earth like a bauble.
Their chain reached to a husband's
Cancer, a widow's broken hip, and hauled
Forth out of the depths, hand over hand,

The out-of-reach dying, the fallen-
And falling-to-pieces. You might shrug
At this quaint belief and its presumption,
Unless you'd felt, as they each had, its tug.

Snoring

There's an explanation for everything, even the need to explain.

Take, for example, the summer I lived with my father in an old folks
home.

He had a new job, running the place, and we lived in a room,

My mother 300 miles away trying to sell our house.

I was nineteen and learned on the first night what a powerful snorer
he was

And also how well she'd trained him. Eventually I thought I'd
discovered

Their spiritual bond or that I'd unlocked a spiritual power.

All eventually explained away by a friend. But let me testify first

To my dawning awareness that either the mind and its intangible
reach

Or an energy greater than anything so material had entered me—

Entered and extended from me. I thought I'd found

The bond between my parents, or one strand of it, one element of the
glue,

Which even then, that summer, was breaking down, unstable after
years of stability.

He snored, his motor chuff, dog honk and blare woke me, and I rose,

Went to his bed across the room, shook him and said, "You're
snoring!"

It wasn't like Samuel shaking Eli awake, asking, "Did you call me?"

But one night

I learned that throwing my legs out of bed would silence him. A snort and a sigh

And he was mute. The room closed its lids to the rich dark of slumber.

It took the whole summer but I discovered what years of bed fellowship had taught him.

And one night, waking to his thundering rumble, I simply thought, "Stop." He stopped.

That summer we drove home to Mother on weekends, talking theology. He told me

His theory of heaven, or rather what happened, he thought, when we died,

For there was a good deal of dying that summer, it being one of the pastimes at the other home.

His theory was based on First John Chapter Four Verse Eight. He that loveth not, knoweth not God,

For God is love. At death, he believed, Love greets us and depending

On our knowledge of love, we either return the greeting or find ourselves at a loss.

∞

Years later, after I told him this story of my parents' former harmony,

And how that summer my father and I had roomed together, and, I

    should add,

How I worked all day on the home's maintenance crew,

Painting the vacated rooms and moving death-beds into storage,

The friend I told my story to explained that a simple change of

    breathing in the room I shared with my father

Would have signaled him to stop. I thought I had moved in the spirit,

With a spirit body and its lithe array of senses, limber knowledge-

    gatherers,

Kinetic fliers like and unlike thought, like but faster than light, that

    wondrousness.

I had lain in the dark amazed that I could affect someone with a

    thought.

Only to have this wonder explained away quite sensibly, yes, it had to

    be true, quite rationally.

And besides my parents' spiritual bond had long been broken, without

    my help or hindrance.

And as for heaven, what of those who never loved because they were

    never loved,

The loveless and unlovable, in who knows what state of snoring-
   repellent life?
When they die, either they find the arousal, the constant arousal of
   love,
Glaring them in the face, shaking them with its welcome, and do not
   understand.
Or they find another welcome, the rich dark of slumber, which passes
   all understanding.

In the Rose Garden

There we shall rest and see, see and love, love and praise. This is what shall be in the end without end.

St. Augustine, *The City of God*

After she had had her operation
And they went to the famous rose garden
Overlooking the city, she in her post-op turban,
He with the keys to the rental car,

They looked out at the rain-gray city,
Sitting on a towel on a wet bench
Among the late roses and those just coming
As the ragged cumulus sailed west.

Little had changed, though they both hoped
That the bad weather had cleared up
In her skull, that she had walked forth
Newly alive from the grave of her condition.

The rose garden dwelt in its self-absorption.
The city's towers looked after the sailing clouds.
The turban of silk scarf the mother wore
Was red as one or two roses holding on.

∞

And the son was pleased to see that.

That moment together, before the lovely city,

Loving each other in the aftermath,

With praise for such a place, praise and the sense

That it would have to end in a little while,

Gave them their pleasure among the roses,

Most of them stalky skeletons and twigs

To tell the truth, which they did not wish to tell.

Encounter

nuda genu nodoque sinus collecta fluentes
The Aeneid, Book I, line 320

Aeneas, lost in the Libyan forest, met his mother Venus

And thought she was some girl, out hunting with Diana.

Virgil describes her naked knee, her flowing garment hitched up by a
    knot.

She offered directions and assurance. Distracting beauty—

You wonder how the hero could go on. Pious Aeneas. He was
    preoccupied.

But as she sped away, he knew her and cried out.

I meet my mother in her youth whenever I see her old.

Isn't this the way with everyone we've loved all our lives?

Endowed with sunlight, her gaze like a bow ready to fire—

And then the bow becomes her sturdy walker, her gaze clouds.

A California girl, she has thrown on a patio dress

And waits for me on her long sofa, out of breath.

She wonders if it's I she's seeing now, that son of hers,

As if I, not she the goddess, were the one disguised.

Monday

Good Lord! the day
    Looked dismal
        Up ahead.

And then the naked
    Biker swept
        Into view,

Smiling toward
    The gas station
        On my right

As I turned left,
    Pausing
        To let him pass

With his gleaming
    Belly, goggles,
        Bearded grin,

And the woman,
    Naked too,
        Seated behind him,

∞

Embracing him,
  Her breasts
    Against his back—

Adam and Eve
  On a Harley
    Davidson.

Even driving
  To hell,
    Who wouldn't smile?

And where I was
  Going wasn't
    As bad as that.

To a Brainy Child in Distress

Dear mind, suffering far away,
I am writing to you on the other side of the earth.

Belovèd thinker, dwelling on no thought
But pain and the pain of thinking, of the mind,

My mind is on you now. My thoughts,
Lit by a dawn you will not see for hours,

Are with you in your darkness, far away.
I hope it is the darkness of deep sleep,

Dear mind. Belovèd thinker, I hope you wake
Far from estranging trouble, home again

To a good thought, a changed mind.

Ending with a Line by Curtis Mayfield

Your beauty has not faded, but mine has.

Though that's immodest—any I had has.

And you fill me with wonder that you'd kiss

An old man as you kissed a boy like this,

The boy you found acceptable when you

Were a girl, beautiful as you are now.

Has age deluded us? It has beguiled

So many. Yet who wants to be a child?

Sometimes I think eternity is looking

Forever forward and thinking nothing ever

Changes at all, nothing at all will change.

And then I see us both standing together

Still, where we kissed each other the first time.

I want to go there, through the sweetness of time.

Last Walk at Home

So I went down to the beach at dusk,
And while I walked along the tide line
Below the beach-crowding summer homes
In a stretch where I did not belong,
The migrating whale lifted its head
Above the shore break and looked around.
I swear I think it looked right at me
With its hieroglyphic eye and asked—
No, not for help, though it was too close.
I turned to the decks of drink parties
And shouted, surf-drowned, across the sand,
Turned back and the whale was gone, all gone,
Back to deep water, back to the tricks
Of twilight, departure, and desire.
And yet the gray oblong eloquence
Of the whale's head, raised above the surf,
Remains with me, like a held-fast dream.
And when I look in memory's eye,
The whale's eye, in its ring of muscle,
Lives again and assures me again
That no matter how many leavetakings
There will be other homecomings.

R. S. Thomas

To see heaven as a length of seashore
And months of bird watching. To stalk the fells
Like a stork trying to get aloft.
To hear wind and river both as voices
And the word *Christ* like a skin of ice
Crackling under shrill, December stars.
One day a week to lift the host
And fortified wine. To have water the rest,
And mutton, cold mutton, mutton stew,
A kipper on Friday, and the desk for poems
And a space of lamplight for the eyes,
Wife and child, like farmers in the combes,
Elsewhere with their own preoccupations,
One God for the drowsy villagers
In the matte black pews, and another,
True God, for the squealing curlew
And the red kite on her found nest.

Dispatches from Devereux Slough

Black Phoebe

Highwayman of the air, coal-headed, darting

Plunderer of gnat hordes, lasso with beak—

"Surely, that fellow creature on the wing,"

The phoebe thinks, "should fly like this."

And loops

His flight path in a wiry noose, takes wing

Like a cast line and hits the living fly,

Ripping it from the fluid of its life.

Devereux Lagoon

Shiners leap ahead of diving cormorants

And killdeer cry, alarming one another.

In an egret's beak, the catch flashes like shook foil.

How well these field glasses scope out the place—

A kestrel sky, serrations of the Madres,

And sand flats darkened by a rare rain shower.

Such an odd peace, as creatures stalk each other.

Dispatch from Devereux Slough

Fall, 2008

The gulls have no idea

The distant bark of sea lions gives nothing away.

The white-tailed kite flutters and hunts.

The pelicans perform their sloppy angling.

The ironbark eucalyptus dwells in ignorance and beauty.

And the night herons brood in their heronry like yoga masters, each
balanced on a twig.

The world has changed. The news will take some time to get here.

From the Garden Toad

A *cri de coeur* of mud, a heartfelt groan
Of deep damp, mother rainfall and her sire;

A plea from underground, from drooping shade,
From memories of sunlight and clear water;

Reproach of an old grandparent half-forgotten—

All in that voice, announcing a desire
To have sex under the giant philodendron.

Marine Layer

No one is out tonight, but just in case,

A tubaphone's deep echo, like a seine net,

Sweeps under darkness and pulls darkness in

The way a trellis shadow cages light.

To hear the foghorn is to hear your childhood,

If you were lucky to have lived near ocean,

Moving again into your neighborhood.

Overcast on Ellwood Mesa

Hawks like it. Wings cast no shadow, hovering,

And white-crowned sparrows are easier to pick out

Among the foxtails, scurrying like mice.

Under the gray cloud cover, blue birds course

Like running water through the fennel stalks,

And the shrike, color of the sky, keeps watch

From the barbed wire of the startling green golf course.

September Song

Those phosphorescent shoulders of the night surf
Passing beneath the pier,

                    as we looked down,

Were an agitation in the falling water
Of creatures set to glowing,

                    all together,

By sudden apprehension, which we perceived
As incandescent wonder,

                    our eyes feasting,

Our hearts filled by the light of crashing down.

Shorebreak, 3 a.m.

At night the swell and crash, the swell and crash,
As waves rush forward, peak, and then collapse
Gasping and giving up a ghost of spray,
Sounds from a distance like a low-voiced hush.

Awake, alone, at the right hour to hear it,
That hush, for all the sleeplessness behind it,
Can lead one, walking wounded, back to sleep.

Sundowner

Waking at nightfall like the other monsters,
The vampire and the moonstruck wolfman, arson
Is hardly required to set your body burning,

Thirsting for dryness, dry brush, stucco houses.

Flame wind, ember wind, wind of moonlit smoke,
Rolling a fog of ash downhill to sea,

The sun's down is the harsh fur of your burning.

Surgeons

The egret is more patient than any watcher
And lances its incision when its stillness
Has made one look away.

                              Its anesthetic
Is stillness, and it numbs the water's skin.

The pelican takes a hatchet to the water,
The egret plies a scalpel.

They extract fish,

But one by smash and gulp, and one by stillness.

The Crystal Ship

Sands Beach, Goleta

The famous rock star thought up his famous rock song

While gazing out at the oil derrick offshore.

Lit up at night it might look, to stoned eyes,

Like a faceted galleon perfect for a song.

Tonight, as sunset gives off its green flash,

The derrick has that look.

      And so does the oil barge

Docked to it, dead black, filling up with cargo.

To a Dead Sea Lion at Sands Beach

You had returned from dry land back to water,

Preferring it, and welcomed the new limbs,

Webbed to conceal your toe and finger bones.

∽

You rolled along the surf, all memory

Of other motion swept back in your wake,

And ended here, among fly-buzzing kelp.

Sleek swimmer drowned,

                    and with your unwebbed bones.

Heaven

When we are reunited after death,

The owls will call among the eucalyptus,

The white-tailed kite will arc across the mesa,

And sunset cast orange light from the Pacific

Against the goldenbush and eucalyptus

Where flowers and fruit and seeds appear all seasons

And our paired silhouettes are waiting for us.

Interesting Times

Everything's happening on the cusp of tragedy, the tip of comedy, the
    pivot of event.
You want a placid life, find another planet. This one is occupied with the
    story's arc:
About to happen, on the verge, horizonal. You want another planet, try
    the moon.
Try any of the eight, try Planet X. It's out there somewhere, black with
    serenity.
How interesting will our times become? How much more interesting can
    they become?

A crow with something dangling from its beak flaps onto a telephone pole
    top, daintily,
And croaks its victory to other crows and tries to keep its morsel to itself.
A limp shape, leggy, stunned, drops from the black beak's scissors like a
    rag.
We drive past, commenting, and looking upward. A sunny morning, too
    cold to be nesting,
Unless that is a nest the crow has seized, against the coming spring.

We've been at this historical site before, but not in any history we
    remember.

The present has been cloaked in cloud before, and not on any holy
  mountaintop.
To know the stars will one day fly apart so far they can't be seen
Is almost a relief. For the future flies in one direction—toward us.
And the only way to sidestep it—the only way—is headed this way, too.

So, look. That woman's got a child by the hand. She's dragging him across
  the street.
He's crying and she's shouting, but we see only dumbshow. Their breath
  is smoke.
Will she give in and comfort him? Will he concede at last? We do not
  know.
Their words are smoke. In a minute they'll be somewhere else entirely.
Everyone in a minute will be somewhere else entirely. As the crow flies.

Good God

Instead of casting them out of Paradise,

Instead of making them labor in pain and sweat,

Instead of instilling tristesse after coitus,

Instead of giving them fire to burn their house down,

And light their way into the outer world,

He could have split them, each with a memory of the other,

And put them each into a separate world.

Bone Fires

The manikin's head is filled with water so
When the bonfire brings it to a boil
It explodes and shoots up into the air—
Not enough water to put out the fire
Which will burn on, consuming the manikin
And itself, throwing its light on the happy faces of the crowd.
They have watched rockets bursting in air
And called back the century when the terrorist Fawkes,
For trying to blow up the government
And unleash a revolt, was hanged, not burned.
The bonfire at this time of year commemorates
A much older terror, the sun weakening,
Dipping out of sight earlier and earlier,
Its worshipers panicking at the darkness
And forcing the darkness back, sending
A message through in a body of fire,
Calling the body of the sun, sometimes
With the bodies of sacrifice—bone fires
Offered like brides to lure the sun to return.
And, indeed, the sun returned, though slowly,
Miserly, through months of desolate cold.
Stoked with bones and piety and the practical sense

That the ritual worked, on the fells of Europe,

The beacon prayers called light to light.

They brought the sun back. The sun returned.

And to gather now around pyres of memory

Upon memory, bundled and stacked and ignited

At any time, but especially as winter comes on,

Can make the most terrifying event—

Auto-da-fé, crucifixion, choose one—a celebration.

North Sea (1978)

Foreigners

Now, in the stone kitchen,
The open honey jar is clotted with wasps;
A thin breeze chills the house
But we keep the window open.

Now we can take a little
From this place, having got through our first winter here.

Nights when the walls of hollow cinder block
Poured dust down through themselves
And the chimney flues blew out their gags of newspaper,
All the lights went on; we hurried
To the living room and waited.

Next door, in white cardigan and sun hat,
The widow comes to the garden wall and leans
Awkwardly over. She shows us the chink
Where the wasps have stuck their nest.
She offers us a cup of plaster
To close it, which we take.

Her lips are full and blue,
Her fingernails blue. Though we think

Her heavy arms and face

Have strength, we wonder,

Watching the wasps hover near their sealed hive,

If she will live much longer

Or, at least, as long as we live here.

We Dare Not Go A-Hunting

Children, here

We call this widow's soap,

This film of soot

On the tile grate,

And this flaw in the window glass

You can peek through

Like a needle's eye

We call the Devil's pupil—

See how it distorts

The garden. The border stones

Of the rosebed

Are thrush's anvils.

Listen, you can hear

The snail crack.

The bird will gobble

The soft insides.

It's just a bird.

But that wingbeat raising

It above the chimneys

Has a name—nestling's hour

Or man fear;

It depends on your mood.

When your breath in your own house

Steams from cold

And the tinkers knock

On your back door

With dry pussy willows

Begging shoes,

We call it winter burdens.

Don't be afraid

To send them away.

Only birds fear them,

Dart from their sticks

And stones. They'll curse

You and you'll want

To track them to their camps—

Wasted, tin shack, smoky

Places on the town's edge.

Let them have their disrespect.

Where they live soot

Is only soot on their faces,

Their soap is lye,

And they have ugly, simple

Names for hunger.

Planting

We are playing what our friend played

On the sea cliff: not falling.

It's a game where we walk the peaked

Mortar. Embedded gravel nicks our shoe heels.

And the wall, like a walk you dream of

In a bad dream, stretches out

From the coal bin to the end of the garden.

We won't fall. It's rhubarb on one side,

A plaster vase of bulbs on the other.

The factory chimney smears a black chalk line down the sky.

The day that boy crawled above us,

Delicate as a lizard, up the pigeon-holed cliff,

Dark blue in his school blazer and shorts,

We watched till the castle keep at the top

Melted him in shadow. How could he have fallen?

As if a trick had occurred

Like a blue bush from a hat, we turned

Our cricked necks to catch the magic

And he was down. A rain of torn clay

Pattered around us on the wet sand.

∞

So, we are careful, remembering mainly

The way he mastered a wall—he could do it!

When you fall, rhubarb crunches like sugar.

When I fall, the plaster vase shatters

And the bulbs that the widow kept warm all winter

Spill over flagstones, ready for planting.

The Close

This is a good road to climb,

If wind is rising with you.

Behind are the park and bomb shelter,

Shelled chestnuts and those

Still in their husks,

And the darkening steps leading down.

My book satchel creaks on my shoulders,

Making me feel their width,

How little they warm my neck.

What small steps I take

Against the wind, past the church door.

In the chancel the flags hang still,

Like old dresses, piecing apart.

Up ahead three roads meet

And the swing shift is coming so quickly

The men appear seamless.

Their faces exude holy oils, flammable—

But that is just twilight.

There I'm as good as home.

A woman cries, "I shouldn't wish it colder!"

And blows past toward the factory gates,

Stork-crooked into the smoke.

Torn posters slap at themselves,

Blues and yellows scabbed with paste.

A dustman challenges with his wide broom

Then offers candy in sticks like chalk.

I eat what I take.

Already I've hummed an old song

Along the graveyard fence.

A family, all in black wool,

Who asked me for streets

With names like rivers I'd read of,

Has gone off swearing they'll soon be home.

Their cheeks were the color of eggs

Held to candles. I said,

"You can take this way."

They answered, "That's where we came from."

Let me tell you, though, I made it home.

There was wind in the close, as always,

Bearing down between wall top and roof top,

Untying sweet pea tendrils.

I rubbed my feet on the mat,

And voices, first sharp

Then forgetting themselves,

Bloomed around me in the warm kitchen.

My Parents Have Come Home Laughing

My parents have come home laughing

From the feast for Robert Burns, late, on foot;

They have leaned against graveyard walls,

Have bent double in the glittering frost,

Their bladders heavy with tea and ginger.

Burns, suspended in a drop, is flicked away

As they wipe their eyes, and is not offended.

What could offend him? Not the squeaking bagpipe

Nor the haggis which, when it was sliced, collapsed

In a meal of blood and oats

Nor the man who read a poem by Scott

As the audience hissed embarrassment

Nor the principal speaker whose topic,

"Burns' View of Crop Rotation," was intended

For farmers, who were not present,

Nor his attempt to cover this error, reciting

The only Burns poem all evening,

"Nine Inch Will Please a Lady," to thickening silence.

They drop their coats in the hall,

Mother first to the toilet, then Father,

And then stand giggling at the phone,

Debating a call to the States, decide no,

And the strength to keep laughing breaks

In a sigh. I hear, as their tired ribs

Press together, their bedroom door not close

And hear also a weeping from both of them

That seems not to be pain, and it comforts me.

Kicking the Candles Out

I have sat below a platform in Scotland,

In a cold room where Sunday school met,

And overhead watched the men dancing,

Their thighs flexing the beat

Into their waists, their arms curled like antlers,

And their women, as good dancers as they,

As muscular and light, shouting.

Hours of music I can no longer hear

Keeps them sweeping their boot toes

So near the ceiling, with its cracks and rain-patches,

That they graze the lights hanging on chains,

Making them turn in a drizzle of plaster

Slowly as planets, and keeping them turning.

Goodbye to a Poltergeist

Like an empty socket alone
On a long baseboard, nothing connects
With him anymore. The bundled family
Has tramped away with its suitcases.
In the spots where he hid he finds light.
To him the dust, with nothing to settle on,
Is a dreary rain.

His push-and-pull with the household gods
Is over; his own knocking rattles him.
His squatter's rights continue but how
To assert them with no one living to gibber at,
No sleeping ear to enter
Or hot brain to poach his eye, the nightmare?

Perhaps, he never existed.
Perhaps, with new residents he will find himself
No longer himself; some unfamiliar dampness
Under a bed will expel him,
A fresh draft blow him deep between floorboards.
He is slowly unfolding, like a crumpled paper
Left in a closet, inanimately with a faint creak.

He needs the children who lived here, who are now

Releasing rolls of streamers from a boatside.

What a mess of tape as the bright wheels unspin

And the boat is tugged out.

In their minds, his rooms, his house, his drizzle of dust

In the cleansing light are cut to ribbons

And sink like ribbons, absorbed by the air.

Lullaby for Amy

We are here, in another provisional city,
Talking of places we will live.
Our bed is another world inside
The blocks of Midwestern houses,
The windows each showing the moon
Of a streetlight through Chinese blinds,
Watery reflections on the walls,
Tropical and bland.
The way birds follow weather
We followed circumstance
And wait for it to change.

The earth is a wave that will not set us down.

Last summer our nerves lay down
To sleep a month in the mountains.
One night in two hours of rain
The river, far below us, rose
Around its islands of motels.
A man on the road was picked up
Off his feet, an old couple
Was torn with him, fanned out

With others thirty miles away.
Cars bobbed with headlights on,
Shuddered, and ducked under.

The earth is a wave that will not set us down.

There is a town in Scotland
On the edge of the North Sea. In fall
The carnival unbolts its haywire rides
Along the strand. Night sweeps in
From Norway with the breath of cod.
Candles are set afloat in wash tubs.
With a leaky water gun you snuff three wicks
And win a coconut. I hear the screams
Of prizewinners, smell the cod
On slabs in the High Street markets.
Sixteen years. I have never been back.

The earth is a wave that will not set us down.

Or does wherever we sleep become our home?
I see us walking among castles

That are great mounds and windings

Of wet sand, in the mist of waves

Breaking out of sight.

Like the horn of a lost boat,

A voice says, "Live here

As you used to live."

And it surprises us, so that we stop

And look back at our scar of footprints,

For we have always lived here, in this way.

The Rote Walker (1981)

Greensleeves

So much comes to mind
From the side, like dust
Down blades of sunlight.
Memory shows a morning
Of all the family together,
Palpable through the years—
But only as elbows and cups.

So much comes to pieces
Like the dust, seeking attachments,
Leaning obliquely forward
To get the whole picture
When the edge says, "Not there,
Not there anymore." We haunt
Our own lives, posing,

Or scan our portraits,
Squinting into the glare
Of the background, hoping
A guardian secret attends us.
Everyone out, I touch

The piano and find five notes

Still cling to my right hand.

A scrap of melody,

It is the one piece

I ever played well. My heart

Is still in it, too.

It is possibly this

That I mean. So much meant

To be lost is saved.

Ascension of the Red Madonna

for Michael Kane

She's been gone whenever I looked.

And here, photographed black and white,

She's leaving, as good as gone.

Blurred wings hoist her canopy,

Black of course as if black

Folded all colors into its cloak.

Above the canvas, white,

The rainbow's egg, waits to be filled in,

Burning in arc brisé windows.

She never rose in my life,

But the tearlessness of this act

Is a catechism of joy. Arms

Flung up to her, everyone wants

What she wants—for her to be gone,

Out of the world, out of those

Flamboyant windows where light—

The photographer's blinded plate—

Appearing as nothing is everything.

Glossolalia

It is impressive when
The fit starts
At the intimate gathering
And the guests' hands tremble above
The incoherent child.

It is the best of childhoods
For her, they believe,
This gift of tongues.
Oh to become
As she is!

To let go, loosen
Your tongue, put
The first word there,
Jesus, *Hosanna*,
And let your mouth roll.

Higher and higher, hooked
To her ghost, like
The brooch to her shock of hair,

Her jaw, remnant bone,
Praises forever.

One notes what she becomes,
The unbraided ends
Of her sight, the pink
Mouth invaded
By echoes.

One notes, too, that she
Looks on, she listens, conchlike,
Attributed voices belonging
To others, their own blood-rush
Of hearing.

And when it is over, she
Is put away, looking
Old now, somewhere upstairs.
A hymn is sung.
A prayer said.

∞

But it is not over

On the drive home, Father

And Grandfather must

Swear and counter-swear, flinging

Faiths into separate heavens.

And how impressed one remains,

Though both men grow

Tired and cannot be talked to,

That there are both ecstasy

And the word against it.

Accordion Music

So the butcher can hold his sweetheart close,
The orchestra plays his request.
Weary families crowded at cocktail tables
Perk up when Mama and Papa glide
Onto the floor, after dancing with each of the children.
Tell me, have you ever been happier?

If you have hated your life
For a week or two, at the heavenly dance,
Which requires no partners,
You can waltz, your empty arms full
Of the human odor of happiness.

Among couples who buried their faces
In each other's collars and hair,
I have danced with my face buried like that,
And paused enthralled as the tall couple,
Who knew all the steps perfectly, swept past,
Barely held within each other's arms,
Dancing now so that later sleep
Will taste sweeter. In the heavenly dance
Such dancers please everyone more.

∞

We will take the week

In the stride of dancers

Who have slept well after tonight,

Together and apart, apart and together.

No, I have never been happier.

Todi, Italy, 1979

The Spell

The prophets are being quiet for a spell.

The wind's been sown. The cabinet maker

Downstairs keeps tacking boxes together.

His hammer clatter's neither hopeful

Nor despairing. Always in the interim

We hear hope. The prophets are so quiet

Or all dead. Remember what they were saying?

Yes, and all our resolutions like calendars

Hanging in showrooms with clouded windows.

Why chastise ourselves to make up for their silence?

If they say nothing now, they're at peace, too.

There goes the buzzsaw, now the power sander,

Smoothing out the minutes. A whirlwind of machinery,

Then silence again, of completion or further preparation.

Descriptions of Heaven and Hell

The wave breaks

And I'm carried into it.

This is hell, I know,

Yet my father laughs,

Chest-deep, proving I'm wrong.

We're safely rooted,

Rocked on his toes.

Nothing irked him more

Than asking, "What is there

Beyond death?"

His theory once was

That love greets you,

And the loveless

Don't know what to say.

The Rote Walker

Even upended in surf, propelled
Into sand burning my chin, I still

Revolved the Saturday lesson for
Sunday, scripture washing my throat.

Under palms dwarfed by eucalyptus,
In turn dwarfed by waves, under

Them all, passage crowned passage like hands
Piled on my head.

And what buzzed through foam and light
Always was the deafening blessedness.

Blessèd the first to recite their assignments
For they shall be first to forget.

●

The eucalyptus forgot, let us say,
In passage to California. Grew
Out of shape, corrupt from the heart

To the stony tips of the fruit. The old lumber
Investment dissolved in their incense.

They grew everywhere, part of the breeze,
Recollecting what was important.
And the pineapple palms shed pigeons.
One summer the city's bladesmen cut
Them to stumps. The church eaves among fronds
Filled with feathers, shit, chortling.
No prayer could poison them.

I would look up, walking, dull-eyed with magnified
Verse, and things would be changed.

•

One thing never changed.
The walk never changed.

The echoing phrase
In the hall, under trees.

∞

The stride back and forth
Bringing memory forth.

The arm hooked in my arm.
The voice in my voice.

My father's arm.
His father's voice.

What you inherit in
Turn was inherited.

What you inherit in turn
Was inherited.

●

Blessèd are the pure in heart
For they shall see . . . I didn't want to.

Entering the chancel at night, to practice,
Heaving closed the lectern Bible,

∞

Don't let me have visions.
Don't creak. Don't flash in my face.

And Sunday, only the pigeons' cooing.
And one spider that toiled down a massive

Light beam into a milliner's flower.
That, I could take.

Blessèd was the silence congregating
Nothing but motes, mites. And the pigeons.

Blessèd my blood swamping
The pure heart with ink.

•

The end of the task
Is to forget the task. Now we can stretch,
Loosen the tie that binds,

Unbutton cuffs, bathe like goldfish
In old baptistries, and stop walking.

The angel of no more assignments
Puts chapter and verse
Back in their places
Among the infinite numbers. Even
These verses, recorded to be forgotten.

Complete, we can sleep off the repetitions,
Grow as we wish, like the eucalyptus.

Sleep and completion, blessèd these peacemakers,
Satisfied fathers.

What Child Is This?

Out in the parking lot, preseasonal,
The Christmas carol stops with a car engine.
And the lovely tune it is set to, "Greensleeves,"
Continues, like a dimming light in a radio,
Haunting us as we go on talking to Grandfather.

Hovering like adorers at his chrome crib,
Father and I might make him laugh, if he could stand
Outside his coma, his scrawny doll's body,
Reading the crack in our attention, the worry—
Will he remain like this through Christmas?

He might wonder that himself, waiting for heaven.
But when he sighs and smacks his lips
The sounds are so personal, I jump. And Father,
Snapping on his razor, sighs back to him
A commiserating "Yes," and tells me to keep talking.

And it's like talking to the one-sided past,
Telling him he's released, his God is waiting,
And hearing only his silence, the razor shaving him,
And the old hymn yoked to the older folk song,
The cast-out lover complaining through the holiness.

Far and Away (1985)

Far and Away

For nights like this they forgot the continent.
Why they came or why their parents came
Apparently always had to do with the weather.
They feel so much at home,
Air and skin match so perfectly, elsewhere
Is beside the point.
Here it is Santa Monica, July 4th,
And they pump from the open ends
Of streets, clotting the cliff edges—friends,
Families and loners—a sign of health.

The old ax head, America, cuts
Under surf here, and what is real
Or not turns abstract.
The night curves like a bandshell.
And if to light it up they attack
With fireworks, they can't budge
A thing but their own hearts.
The palms, the gazebos of graffiti—
Be Here Now!—you can imagine all the silly
Trappings, as they look up and down at the dark.

A hundred feet below, the beach is amber

In protective lights and fronts

The ocean's jeweler's velvet. The arc

Of someone's Mexican bottle rocket faints,

After a twisting spurt,

Ghost in a bubble chamber.

Then the big stuff clamors for all eyes,

Leaves no gaps for gasping.

Flower, exfoliation turn into one

Steady miracle of blazing faces.

There is an individual desire

Among them to fire sky-high and rain

In *oohs* and *ahs* and vanish,

Touching no one who could swear

The dissolving lace capping him was ash:

Like the eye's voluptuous looking—just to see—

See what it's like and, scattered

After blossoming, grow

Into one piece again, feel the flow

Of identity, your very own, from foot to head.

∞

On nights like this it's not acceptable

To cough with cold or shiver with irony

At your own home,

Or at the amusement of your family,

Which you must pick up like a telephone,

Even if only to set it back in its cradle.

There they

Stand at the edge night draws from,

Releasing it bombed

And speckled with afterimages. The current theory,

That their coast will drown,

Crack off up to Arizona,

They believe only as a grand occasion

For combustion—redwoods, gas—

And each of them a survivor with the news.

Who wouldn't want to be there then?

Think of the Pacific on that night,

Like a deceptive Spanish dancing skirt

That shimmers and almost seems too short,

But when twirled flares out and fills your sight.

The Supremes

In Ball's Market after surfing till noon,

We stand in wet trunks, shivering,

As icing dissolves off our sweet rolls

Inside the heat-blued counter oven,

When they appear on his portable TV,

Riding a float of chiffon as frothy

As the peeling curl of a wave.

The parade emcee talks up their hits

And their new houses outside of Detroit,

And old Ball clicks his tongue.

Gloved up to their elbows, their hands raised

Toward us palm out, they sing,

"Stop! In the Name of Love," and don't stop,

But slip into the lower foreground.

Every day of a summer can turn,

From one moment, into a single day.

I saw Diana Ross in her first film

Play a brief scene by the Pacific—

And that was the summer it brought back.

Mornings we paddled out, the waves

Would be little more than embellishments—

Lathework and spun glass,

Gray-green with cold, but flawless.

When the sun burned through the light fog,

They would warm and swell,

Wind-scaled and ragged,

And radios up and down the beach

Would burst on with her voice.

She must remember that summer

Somewhat differently. And so must the two

Who sang with her in long matching gowns,

Standing a step back on her left and right,

As the camera tracked them

Into our eyes in Ball's Market.

But what could we know, tanned white boys,

Wiping sugar and salt from our mouths,

And leaning forward to feel their song?

Not much, except to feel it

Ravel us up like a wave

In the silk of white water,

Simply, sweetly, repeatedly,

And just as quickly let go.

∞

We didn't stop either, which is how
We vanished, too, parting like spray—
Ball's Market, my friends and I.
Dredgers ruined the waves,
Those continuous dawn perfections,
And Ball sold high to the high-rises
Cresting over them. His flight out of L.A.,
Heading for Vegas, would have banked
Above the wavering lines of surf.
He may have seen them. I have,
Leaving again for points north and east,
Glancing down as the plane turns.
From that height they still look frail and frozen,
Full of simple sweetness and repetition.

Long-Stemmed Roses

Mist clings tonight,
    And the hiss of passing cars
Is like the release of pressure
    As pressure builds,

As Jody Portillo's Riviera
    Trails his entourage
Into the gym parking lot,
    His first name laced in the rear window. . . .

Everyone was dancing—our girls
    Wore their orchids,
The purple spotted horns,
    On their breasts.

And Jody's car club and their dates
    Held roses in locked hands,
Pumping a locomotion
    Into the red petals.

Noise of rock, and outside,
    Muffled hammers shattered glass,

And the Pacific Ocean
    Breathed its fog.

Everyone was dancing,
    Sheen of black hair and blonde,
Smell of overfragrant colognes
    With songlike and brutal names.

Albums embalm such nights.
    And this one, too, scrawled
By cop light on parchment carbon
    Has kept:

The girls standing apart,
    Brown and white, doused
In the sulfur glare
    Of the street lamps.

And the football team, huddled
    Incongruously, breaking
With a bright shout.
    And the car club ready. . . .

I remember the scent

 Of low tide, Jody Portillo nicked

Under the left nipple

 And the first string center in the thigh,

And feel the thorn on the stalk

 Leading back to such

Blossoms of memory,

 When we were young.

By-blows

They wake like opening sea anemones,
Although none turns into a flower—
Wake with their dew, a salt clamminess
On gritty skin, under the pier.
Above them, boards thump, panels unlock,
Food machines cough. The gaunt morning moon
(Why should they look?) turns blue in the jowl.
From the surf I would watch them climb
The nubbled walk to the library park—
Watch the sun accept if not bless them
As they rose, hung over on cough syrup
Or pop wine—where bladed cacti filled
With sprinkler water, and certain benches
Were somewhat safe. Told to move on,
There was the library, the nook tables
And pillowing books, and after a decent interval,
The discreet voice that spoke.

What did my father tell me? About that one
Who whirled to face an empty window
As we passed on the bare avenue?
They blow into town, beg money, blow out again.

But you know the rest of it.

They taste sand every morning, wake

In flannel grayed with their sweat,

Touch the tide's cold hem, and smell the sunrise.

Planting their fingertips, they can tell

A story as roundabout as any medieval allegory,

With their damp gunpowder stubble,

Their drain-waste of hair,

Their air of illegitimate princes

Double-crossed by sires and stars.

What we see looking at them is what they see

Looking away—the otherness of the moon,

Which we feel no urge to correct.

While You Are Gone I Look for Constellations

It is chaos at first,

Which it truly is,

These fossil lights

Of flyaway stars.

Then the charts

Under my flashlight

Begin to match

What I see. Backward

At first, the Pleiades

Appear west. And then, I see,

And turn to Deneb,

The Swan's tail,

And the Swan angling

Toward the earth.

In an hour of craning

I have it down.

The cold clings

Like a coat of mail.

I name Vega, Altair,

And laugh as I have since childhood

When finding out answers.

Over my shoulder

Orion lugs, on his shoulder,

The giant Betelgeuse,

Coming after the faint Sisters.

Never has he caught up,

Though that axial star

In Cygnus, diving for cover,

Looks like a wound.

Never have I missed

You as I do. I walked

All day through the house,

Into the small town,

Checked out this text

On astronomy for the cover

Packet of star charts,

And waited for night,

For the darkest, clearest part,

And the longest part,

When these stars were

First named in places

Which they have long since left.

Poem in June

My daughter is riding out after rain
    In the undercast light of sunset,
    When the great ash a block away,
    Studded with grackles like fleas,
Turns, for an instant, a color worth
A long meditation on heartbreak. I stop,
    And, astride my shoulders, she gasps
    And sinks fingers into my hair.

So, I save the speech I might have made
    To my two-year-old daughter,
    Saying instead, "Look at the tree.
    How many blackbirds?"
And feel the root-tearing grip in my hair relax
As she trusts me again and responds, "Look at it!
    How many blackbirds!" I count,
    Rolling my shoulders to steady her.

And she trills the numbers off her tongue
    And keeps counting, looping ahead and back.
    Sequence is a thread of grass,
    And the years before she was born

And the years she will outlive her parents

And be herself outlived, can be woven to make,

    However tangled, one network

    Of time to hold this moment.

So, an odd slant of light turns a tree

    Of new leaves the color of fall. Three birds

    Perch there, like an October day.

    So, today, thirty, I can say

How long it takes to grow up. When she is ready,

As children do, she will decide how I lived.

    Now she is riding. And for her,

    As she cups my ears and points my face,

I am a good horse. At the oily creek,

    I watch for fat water moccasins

    And set her down at the edge.

    I claw rocks from mud,

And she pitches them sidearm, underhand, in chance arcs.

They land at her feet, clattering on shingle.

    And they hit home, splashing crowns,

    Briefly clear, from the black surface.

The City in the Sea

Coastal spring. Desert spring.

The air a balm of weightlessness.

Yet the students in their rows

As the light drapes their shoulders

Are writing almost in unison.

My mother is among them.

When they pause,

The whole class trembles.

But I know her trembling.

One hand anchors a page,

The other copies.

This glimpse of my mother's past,

This suburb of Los Angeles—

What am I looking for?

To say the city is a net

Is to number its strands

And exclude much.

To say a bed of kelp,

Swelling and subsiding,

Mazy with eels and sunfish,

Says a little more.

It is a sea, too, and floods

My memory like a basin,

Filling it with salt water,

Its complexity, that will neither

Quench thirst nor wash

Without leaving its residue

But in the end sustains.

My mother's school, her apartment house,

Even the post office

Where her mother works,

Are like aquarium sculpture.

One street binds them all,

Running below magnolias.

As I think of her, those trees

Open and lose their flowers,

Ancient, simple corollas.

A hand spreads wide a petal.

A fingernail engraves it.

The broad evergreen leaves

Give their cold-blooded gleam.

∞

I try to turn that look,

The simple, evergreen gaze,

On myself, too. One night,

Leaving a plain, brick church

And some youth event behind,

I ran with my girlfriend

On that street, under the trees,

Ending in the schoolyard

Where we embraced and kissed.

We had come miles by car

And did not know where we were.

Though I touched her breast

And held her indignant stare,

We both kept kissing.

Why should it have mattered,

Once I learned the coincidence,

To feel as if I had come

Twenty years too late?

But I remember a story.

In a dream, a girl's drowned lover

Speaks to her, two vague words.

Awake, pursuing him,

She boards a ship made of stone,

And as it sinks, becomes a sunfish.

She seeks him only to learn

That her life has saved his,

And now they are both alone.

The two words were *Your Soul*.

When I return to this city

I am always looking for something.

I believe my mother is writing,

In that imagined classroom,

The history of a word.

Old English. Dutch. German.

Old Icelandic. Gothic. *Soul* related to *Sea*.

Related, too, to the future

Where she will tell me stories,

Like that one, and give me a soul,

Believing—of course, believing—

That I will never lose it.

Cavafy in Redondo

Our ruins run back to memory.
Stucco palaces. Pleasure bungalows. The honeycomb
Of the beachcombers' cluster of rentals.
I remember them. Filings in sand
Pricking up at the magnet of nostalgia.
A sigh of dusty filaments. Our ruins
Wear the as-yet-unruined like coral crowns.
Night life blows through the boardwalk's
Conch-shell coils of neon, skirting the water.
This was never—Ask my parents—a great city.
It had its charm, like a clear tidal shallows,
Silted-in now, poldered, substantial, solid,
Set for the jellying quake everyone expects.

I walked these streets one night with a new lover,
An as-yet-to-be lover. It took a whole night
Of persuasion. I had been gone a year
And walked as sea mist compounded the dew.
My legs ached by the time bed was agreed to.
How sentimental it was, to flatter, listen,
Cajole, making little whining endearments,
Plodding ritualistically among landmarks,

Sandy shrines in alleys, the black meccas
Of plate-glass windows fronting the beach
Where white froth reflected in the night.
I kept that ache, not love's, after we parted.

We did not part to history with its glosses.
We were not even footnotes. Our ruins
Will bear out no epics or histories here,
Footprints compounded of dew and fog
And under them, maybe a rusty antique
Which, boiled in acids, will tell a tale.
After all, ships passed, broke up on the point.
Mainly, the beach eroded in great ridges
Until ground cover belted it back. A pleasure dome
Was dismantled, certain fashions
Of dress and of love. History builds to last,
Crumbles to last, shakes off its dust
Under the delicate excavating brush—to last.

Built above the beach was a colossus,
Humped and strutted and roaring with many voices.
Winds chased through it screeching, and then,

It stood silent. People flocked to it, entered it,

And though not lost, screamed as if tortured.

I am joking. There was a roller coaster

Of some note and no small size. Where did it go?

Ah, yes, lost to the coral make-up

Of that teetering lover who walked beside me,

Tired of my harangue, the persuasive underlove

That wanted to rise to the lips, those lips

Colored by fuming street lamps.

Young, my parents drove out from a distant city,

Through tawny hills medallioned with oak.

I have seen their worn postcards of the town,

A tide pool of neighborhoods mantled around

By semi-wilderness and orange groves.

Missiles came to squat above our house

On a benchmarked hill, turned obsolete,

And floated away on flatbeds, ruptured patios in their places.

We, too, left that house that heard,

In every lath and windowpane, the industry of phosphorus,

Grinding out the waves in the late darkness.

My parents—all of us—have come and gone and left

No ghosts here. And that is our good fortune—

To give it all to the ocean, the troubled sleeper.

The Black Riviera (1990)

The Children

The children are hiding among the raspberry canes.

They look big to one another, the garden small.

Already in their mouths this soft fruit

That lasts so briefly in the supermarket

Tastes like the past. The gritty wall,

Behind the veil of leaves, is hollow.

There are yellow wasps inside it. The children know.

They know the wall is hard, although it hums.

They know a lot and will not forget it soon.

When did we forget? But we were never

Children, never found where they were hiding

And hid with them, never followed

The wasp down into its nest

With a fingertip that still tingles.

We lie in bed at night, thinking about

The future, always the future, always forgetting

That it will be the past, hard and hollow,

Veiled and humming, soon enough.

The Black Riviera

For Garrett Hongo

There they are again. It's after dark.

The rain begins its sober comedy,

Slicking down their hair as they wait

Under a pepper tree or eucalyptus,

Larry Dietz, Luis Gonzalez, the Fitzgerald brothers,

And Jarman, hidden from the cop car

Sleeking innocently past. Stoned,

They giggle a little, with money ready

To pay for more, waiting in the rain.

They buy from the black Riviera

That silently appears, as if risen,

The apotheosis of wet asphalt

And smeary-silvery glare

And plush inner untouchability.

A hand takes money and withdraws,

Another extends a plastic sack—

Short, too dramatic to be questioned.

What they buy is light rolled in a wave.

They send the money off in a long car

A god himself could steal a girl in,

Clothing its metal sheen in the spectrum
Of bars and discos and restaurants.
And they are left, dripping rain
Under their melancholy tree, and see time
Knocked akilter, sort of funny,
But slowing down strangely, too.
So, what do they dream?

They might dream that they are in love
And wake to find they are,
That outside their own pumping arteries,
Which they can cargo with happiness
As they sink in their little bathyspheres,
Somebody else's body pressures theirs
With kisses, like bursts of bloody oxygen,
Until, stunned, they're dragged up,
Drawn from drowning, saved.

In fact, some of us woke up that way.
It has to do with how desire takes shape.
Tapered, encapsulated, engineered
To navigate an illusion of deep water,

Its beauty has the dark roots

Of a girl skipping down a high-school corridor

Selling Seconal from a bag,

Or a black car gliding close to the roadtop,

So insular, so quiet, it enters the earth.

Awakened by Sea Lions

They crowd their rookery, the dilapidated outcrop
The ocean gives a bubble-top of glass to at high tide.
Among them two or three of the four-ton elephant seals
Loll pathetically, like queen bees without hives.
The lions call out. Insomniac, late, the fog a loose curtain
Of moonshot aquatic light, restless and static,
    They speak.

But not to us. Nor to the ocean. I have heard
One daughter wake on her top bunk sobbing
And her younger sister below ask her what's wrong.
Deep in the night, all of us waking to her cry.
"What's wrong?" And then, "I can't sleep."
Just the two of them. Silence again. Slumber.
    The call comes

Out of the vast, peaceful sea rimmed by new worlds.
And those who hear it are soothed, even though
It might rise from throats that gulp pale fish
Torn out of the wave, from inelegant chimeras
    With limbs like dolphins',

Dog-eared, whiskered like cats, mouths set
With human teeth. The call travels its distance.
Once heard, it travels further.

The Shrine and the Burning Wheel

On the way to the evening reading,

Stopped at a Quick Stop for cigarettes,

I saw, as did everyone parked there

Or passing, a gang of boys,

    Local boys probably,

Burning the front wheel of a ten-speed.

The bicycle, turned upside down,

Stood on the dumpster side of the store,

And one boy glanced from the corner

    Through the front window.

    Transcendence—that's what

It means to want to be gone

As, turning the eye's corner

To the sudden glare of fire,

The local terror stares in your face.

    I got the hell out of there.

And kept the spidery intaglio

Of the one, their lookout, peeping

Into the store window at—it must have been—

    The boy who owned the bicycle

    In his clerk smock

    Making change from the safe.

At the evening reading, as the poet was

Introduced at length, she rested her head

On the heel of her left hand,

Full hair falling to the propped elbow,

And, as the prologue ran on,

Shook a little dandruff from her hair.

And what I saw was no longer her gesture

But the memory of Nora and Bo Dee Foster

And the crowd at the Shrine Auditorium

In Los Angeles, long ago, listening

To "Renascence" and "A Few Figs from Thistles"

And one that rhymed "stripèd pants" and "Paris, France."

Bo Dee remembers how

As Huxley went on

And on introducing her,

Edna Millay shook the dandruff from her hair.

Transcendence is not

Going back

To feel the texture of the past

Like the velvet nap of the loges

In the Shrine. It is wanting to be

Anywhere else.

Clearly, I don't understand.

The wheel spins. It is not hard to ignite

The hard lean tire with lighter fluid.

It flashes and a round of smiles

Breaks in the dismal circle

    Of the boy pack

    From the apartment complexes.

In their stripèd pants they open doors

Of sedans to men in maroon fezzes.

But they are men themselves, Nobles,

And wear ruby rings set with diamonds

    And symbols.

Searchlights mortar the clear night.

"Thank you, Noble," says one man

Helping his wife to the curb.

    She, white as a fez's tassel,

    And the grandchildren

Will see a Chinese girl prodigy at the piano,

Jugglers on unicycles,

And, the reason they've come,

    Edgar Bergen and Charlie McCarthy,

    Aging and never to age.

Here at the Shrine, with its swag tent ceiling

And Arabic signs, hands of the crowd

> Grip in ways

> That cannot be revealed.

> But now the amps are on.

Big Brother and the Holding Company are on.

The rapid fire of strobes cuts, cuts.

But that's too much, too soon.

> Instead, it's the Boy Scout Expo.

> Let it be calm for a while

As it would be at a state fair

Inside a great pavilion.

> Here are the Scouts displaying

> Their skill at fly casting.

> The arc ends in a splash.

Fly-blue or fly-green, it hits the pool

Among the crowd, under the roof

Of the Shrine Hall. There is quiet.

Then a cheer. Now the speakers start up.

> Janis Joplin, shapeless and small,

In the loose madras fabric of her dress,

Flares and thrashes in the wind

Her body makes to the music,

Cut and cut and cut

By the strobe lights across her hair.

Transcendence is what she wants

Or not what she wants, to live

In the world or out of it,

To be anywhere else

Or here, as a studied voice

Says its poetry of heaven and earth,

And meshed with it, hidden,

A wheel of history turns,

And the boys burn the wheel.

Days of '74

What was the future then but affirmation—
The first *yes* between us,
Followed by the first lingering dawn?
Waking below a window shaded by redwoods
(Waking? We hadn't slept—),
We found time saved, like sunlight in a tree.

Still, the house was cold, and there were shadows.
The couple in the next room
Rapped the wall to quiet us, like them,
Condescending from a bitter knowledge
That, young as we all were,
Love didn't last, but receded into silence.

Wedging our pillows back of the headboard
That clapped in time with us,
We let them think we agreed. Then, holding on,
We closed each other's mouths and felt that slowness
Which the best days begin with
Turn into the speed with which they fly.

Flight was that year's theme, all around us—
Flight of hunter and hunted,

The President turning inward on one wing,

And, on the patio, the emigration

Of termites, a glittering fleet,

Leaving that shadowed house a little lighter.

Within it all, above it, or beyond,

We thought we were the fixed point,

And held still as the quail lit down beside us

And waited for her plump mate to appear,

His crest a quivering hook.

The valley's reach of sunshine reeled them in.

There was wilderness around us, don't forget.

Behind the nets of fragrance

Thrown across our path by the acacia

Lurked the green man or the kidnapper.

And there was the Pacific

With its own passions taking place as rain.

The sorrow of the couple in the next room

Was a deep muteness nightly.

That loneliness could come of loving was

Like news of time cored out of the redwood.

The house that we made shake,

Or thought we did, was taking wing already.

After we left, still it took us years

Before we stopped comparing

Every morning together to that first one

And every place we lived to that first place

And everything we said

To that first word repeated all night long.

Good Friday

Heat is what I imagine, dust and tension,

And by midafternoon the cloudburst,

The sudden coolness, a balm for some, none

For those who had seen a loved one die,

Horribly, nails through his wrists, suffocating,

If not bleeding to death, in the heat, the tension.

The rain covered the gap of his life,

A rattling screen of iridescent beads

Pummeling the dust, cutting off our view.

It does no good to forecast the weather

Backward. If it was tempest weather,

The nails bit the wood thirsting for sap,

The grain split with a hoarse cough.

Then, rain fell. The woods filled with freshness.

Sandal thongs gleamed. Faces basked.

Verisimilitude is magic. Jesus struggled

For breath, hanging forward, and said little.

Then, someone prodded him, but he was dead.

He lived. He died. He knew what was happening.

The night my father came home from Claremont

And sat at the foot of my bed, forcing up

The news of D.'s death, was a Good Friday.

D.'s bowels had locked and starved his brain

Of blood. He died screaming, and in silence.

There were no last coherent words.

And his young wife (both of them so young)

Had curled between his deathbed and the wall.

All this my father told me.

And the story of D.'s life was told,

Friend by friend, a dozen lives.

A year later there was a gathering

To view home movies of him, and a film

He'd made, mostly a lyric reel

Of widening water circles—

Loved because his eye had seen them,

Turned the lens to ingest the light.

D. died when I was sixteen. I remember

His twenty-fourth birthday, his last,

The strobe lights' percussion, Zorba music,

And him dancing because that was the soul:

Rhythmless, bare-chested, leaping in air,

Really, I think, in all the sweat and shouting,

To prove a man could dance that way,

In a church basement, a man could

With another man, their wives clapping.

They say that Jesus died at thirty-three.

They say so, and now I think I believe it.

Never have my age and others' ages

Seemed so real, so physically what they are.

I see the skin's grain, the back's curve,

The pools of stamina drawn carefully

To contain the world no longer vast

In possibilities, except that it

Can kill, even in your prime.

And yet, thirty, a craftsmen in wood,

One finally thought he knew what humankind

Wanted—to be loved, to be forgiven,

Which meant to be loved always.

And yes, perhaps, he was a little naive.

He believed that this was possible,

Loved as he had been by his mother,
His father who trained him to work wood.
He knew the feel of love's grain, its texture.

Knew a way, too, to speak of love.
It had a substance, a heft, like wood
Or nets or sacks of seed or jars of ointment.
Things came to mind, they came to hand,
Unscrolling even from the written word.
The world was made of love, to love.
And he was on the road, finding listeners.
And he was of an age when he knew doom
Waited for him, that people heard what they wanted.

That is, they heard what they lacked.
The glory of it turned the desert green.
The cedars' vertical aspiration said it.
Roads offered their dust, their thieves.
Cities congregated suspiciously, busy
And explosive with potential. Teacher,
They called him (as they called others):
Everyone must be included, loved,
The excluded most of all, who would doom him.

∞

They say he taught three years. They say
Much about him, that his life
Was seamless, like his robe.
And, yet, he was that age when,
Seamed, you put away childish things
And take children into your arms.
They would doom him. He entered rooms
Forbidden to be entered, where the dead lay,
Rising at his call, to doom him.

Heat is what I imagine, dust and tension.
The scourging I imagine he understood,
The soldiers' reviling, surely he had seen that,
And the way crucifixion worked, the need to
Break legs to bring the strangulation on.
(No need in his case. He'd already gone.)
In the cloudburst, the downpour of signs,
The saints out walking, puzzled to be raised,
Things were torn, shattered, mystifying.

Today, the lawns are clouded with at least
Six kinds of wildflower. Ground ivy,

Corn speedwell, henbit, chickweed,

Spring beauties, and the dandelion.

My daughters know their names. My wife

And I look at them, the girls and flowers,

And none of us thinks of him, who does not

Haunt us, any more than anyone gone,

When there is such a theodicy of blossoms.

Our four-year-old's lips nearly touch

A dandelion globe, spluttering,

As she learns to blow the seeds away.

One night, the sepals close on golden petals.

Then, open changed. Gone to seed.

Gone to worlds of possibility.

What's love, even eternal love,

But evolution to endure? And doesn't it

Begin here, learning to blow a kiss?

Yes, it is complex, I know.

Look at the articulation of the seed itself,

The filament erect to its parachute

Of downy hairs. How easily

It could be taken as almost cruciform.

How willingly the wind could explicate it:

His breath. His sign. But it is ours,

As we show her how to force the air

Out in a rush, our love she takes as her own.

The Gift

When I was five my father kidnapped me.
He didn't keep me long enough to worry
My mother. And I wonder if she knew.
But I knew, five years old. That day at school,
He waited for me at the double doors,
His Hudson parked behind him, ready to go.
I knew he'd come when he was not supposed to.
He said it was all right, my mother knew.
On the front seat, there was a present for me,
And as he started, he said I could unwrap it.
The ribbon wouldn't give, the gift box buckled.
But he was driving, couldn't stop to help.
Outside the windshield traffic lights hung down
From cables, and the bushy tops of palms
Showed up at intervals that I could count.
A pink or yellow building front skimmed past.
But mostly I could only see the sky.
A child could hardly see from those old cars
With the window set up high above your shoulder.
The sky went by, pale blue and white and empty,
Crossed suddenly by wire. And I gave up
Trying to take the wrapping off my present

Until we reached wherever we were going.

Then, at a stop, one of those tall palm trees

That wears a shaggy collar of dead fronds

Leaned down and opened up the door and stepped in

Beside me. Daddy called her Charlotte dear

And said that I was Susan. Sitting down,

She was the tallest woman, and she wore

A high fur collar with white points of hair.

She let me put my hand on them. So soft!

I was excited then, because she helped me

Unwrap my gift and set me on her lap

So I could see. It was a long drive then,

Through orange groves where all the fruit was green,

Past dairy farms that you could smell right through

The rolled-up windows and even through the strength

Of Charlotte's perfume and Daddy's after-shave.

We went down through a canyon to the beach,

And Charlotte pointed at a pair of wings,

Two bars of black and white that drifted high

Above the gap. She said it was a condor.

Against the ocean, where the canyon ended,

A roller coaster's highest hump rose up.

Beside it was a dome with colored flags.

By this time in the afternoon, at home,

Mother would listen to the radio

And pretty soon I'd have to go indoors

For dinner. Daddy bought me a corn dog,

An Orange Julius, and for dessert—

The biggest cotton candy in the world.

But first I rode the carousel three times.

From there, as I pumped slowly up and down,

I had a good look at the two of them.

Daddy, like a blond boulder, round and bald.

And Charlotte, though I knew how soft she was,

Like a palm tree still, looking stiff and spiky.

I knew he loved me (maybe she did, too),

But soon he'd have to take me home to Mother.

Around us broke a bank of evening fog,

Softly but coldly, too. We had to leave.

Later I fell asleep on Charlotte's arm,

Her fox fur floating lightly on my hair

And Daddy's present open on my lap.

I wish I'd kept awake to have my say

That day, that one day clearer than all my childhood.

Next morning I awoke in my own bed,

And Mother asked if I'd had fun with Daddy.

He'd kidnapped me. She didn't seem to know it!

Daddy and Charlotte never married. Mother

Went on as if he were a kindly neighbor

Dropping in now and then to help her with me.

We'll see if that's the way I treat your father.

I can't recall what the gift was he gave me.

Miss Urquhart's Tiara

For Chase Twichell

I know this can't mean anything at all,

Except I found the fringed phacelia

Today, walking with my daughters beyond

The baseball diamond, and remembered reading

A story called "Miss Urquhart's Tiara"

So long ago, remembering it surprised me,

Like the Smoky Mountain flower shading white

To the pale blue of skies this time of year,

All the way from the mountains four hours east.

From one flower clouds amassed.

The story built its paragraphs.

And the grass, thick as the stumbling talk

That goes on in my head, tripped me here and there,

As when I'm alone I fall into speech.

(The habit worries me, when I can see myself

As an old man snarled in monologues.)

The fringed phacelia. Miss Urquhart.

Strange, their names meant nothing to each other.

Or to my daughters. The toddler doubled

Over a tuft of grass she hugged for balance.

Her older sister drifted at the edge

Of calling range, the fringe of cottonwoods
Along the stream that cuts our neighborhood
And draws the network nobody thinks of
Except in flood, except the city planner
Who, I imagine, knows the map by heart
Like his palm's creasework. All it is is drainage,
Though clear weather clears the water,
And clams, crayfish, snails with turbinate shells
Come to life. There's a faint tinge of odor,
And up the bank, a humped concrete manhole
Reads "Sanitary Sewer." We don't care.
I showed the little one the blue-white flower.
She took it, put it in her mouth, and ate it.
Her sister called. The poplar she stood under
Was the spine of a green book I reached for.

The story of "Miss Urquhart's Tiara,"
Which I hold open in my lap somewhere
On a peninsula, in a hotel,
In a fall noted there for peaks of color
Washed out by rain, was written by someone
You often find in such anthologies,

Reserved for rain in hotels on peninsulas—
Stevenson or Saki, Maugham or Kipling.
In it, two children, brother and sister,
Take a walk one spring day with their teacher.
(It may be Scotland, it may be Stevenson.)
It's a long walk, but the children keep up
For the first mile. The road's border of nettles
Prickles the boy's bare legs. His sister pales.
A heavy dew crowns weeds and spiderwebs,
And there's a taste of steam in the air.
The sky looks like a pane of whitewashed glass.

Wide-shouldered and wide-eyed, their smiling friend,
Miss Urquhart, urges them, reaching a hand
To each. Soon they will leave their native land
For—India? (Kipling?)—for a distant country.
And she wants them to have a memory
Of such a day as this that will filter back
Through another climate's heat waves and dust.
But when the children learn it's two miles yet,
They add a whine to the field's insect drone.
Thirsty—they're thirsty. She finds them stalks

Of timothy to chew. They're both too big

To be carried and yet still young enough

To want to be, saying their daddy would.

On they plod. And Miss Urquhart slowly sees

This outing as a bad job, proposed for

The parents' sake, grateful, interesting people,

Wound up in packing twine, and for the children,

Wilting and peevish now, but who adore her.

The girl plops down, defeated, in her jumper.

The boy scratches his legs. Miss Urquhart pulls him

Dockweed leaves to rub them, then tells why

They have to keep walking and not turn back.

Ahead there is a church—oh, they don't care!

Once, I was to be married there, she says.

Now, this is a secret, you can't tell.

But if you'll walk with me, you'll hear it.

Are you married, Miss Urquhart? they both ask.

No, and that doesn't matter one bit now.

I want to see this church again. But if

I tell you why, you have to listen and keep up.

No more bubbling babies. Now, take my hands.

There's a town, too, where we can have our tea.

And she tows the children through it all—

The landscape, the fatigue, the tale she tells.

Hedges back away to give them room.

The dew dries. Nettles reach but do not touch.

She was engaged, a long, long time ago,

To the headmaster of the little school

There, where they are going. She was his first.

Whereas, she'd had boyfriends. How many boyfriends?

Boys at church, at school, at dances, boys

To walk with on this very road to town,

Which there, you see, is cropping up just now.

And there's the church, that tuft of sooty stone.

And that's the church where you were to be married?

Yes, and I even know the pastor still.

He'll give us tea. And why were you not married?

You know, she says, not everybody must be.

You can be very happy all alone.

And are you very happy, Miss Urquhart?

I am, very. And why were you not married?

He went away, to Australia. I stayed.

They step into the small, cool church, and meet

The pastor, who gives them tea and takes them home.

He went away because he was not loved.

He gave her a tiara, to wear on their honeymoon

In the capital—Edinburgh or London.

The little crown had been a great-aunt's bequest

To him for his bride. He gave it to her

Too soon, it seems, because he asked for it back.

Then, gave it again, set it on her head.

Then, asked for it back, left for Australia.

You can be very happy all alone.

But this part, winding through her on the ride back,

Never reaches the children's ears. She catches

Her breath, repeating, "Gave. Then, took. Gave."

Had she said it aloud? No one had noticed.

She leaves the children touchingly, says farewell

To the grateful, interesting parents,

And turns back into the hidden channels

Of her story. Not is she happy, but how

Did he, who loved her, make himself happier?

∞

The last time they sat up late in her room,

The window held the summer's hour of darkness,

And they were silent, watching through this night

That would end soon, an easy vigil, when,

Speaking to someone else (a dream companion?),

He said, Yes, he had dreamed of Australia

All of his life, the Outback painted

With runes that someday he would read.

Someday. She knew she didn't love him

Enough to tease him for this, but instead,

Thought of the tiara in its hinged box,

The almost satiny pearls, the almost cold

Diamonds, the almost tarnished web of silver

They studded, and the ritual of giving,

Then taking it back to have a stone reset,

A broken silver filament resoldered.

Whatever it was worth, it was enough,

She knew it now, to get to Australia.

She turns away, having told the children

Only enough to keep them satisfied

And us only enough to keep us reading.

The front door closes as she turns away,

The street lamps are lit up, Australia

Is a lost continent. But do you know,

Miss Urquhart, that I remember the cool leaf

Of dockweed rubbing up and down my calf,

And how you trailed us, my sister and me,

Behind you like a wake, how we kept up,

Questioning you just as you'd intended,

And getting for all our curiosity

A cup of tea? Today, among clouds

Of fringed phacelia in the deep grass,

When my daughters heard me speak to someone

They couldn't see, they waited for an answer.

So did I, even though I held their hands.

It took them pressing close to close the book.

Questions for Ecclesiastes (1997)

Ground Swell

Is nothing real but when I was fifteen,
Going on sixteen, like a corny song?
I see myself so clearly then, and painfully—
Knees bleeding through my usher's uniform
Behind the candy counter in the theater
After a morning's surfing; paddling frantically
To top the brisk outsiders coming to wreck me,
Trundle me clumsily along the beach floor's
Gravel and sand; my knees aching with salt.
Is that all that I have to write about?
You write about the life that's vividest.
And if that is your own, that is your subject.
And if the years before and after sixteen
Are colorless as salt and taste like sand—
Return to those remembered chilly mornings,
The light spreading like a great skin on the water,
And the blue water scalloped with wind-ridges,
And—what was it exactly?—that slow waiting
When, to invigorate yourself, you peed
Inside your bathing suit and felt the warmth
Crawl all around your hips and thighs,
And the first set rolled in and the water level

Rose in expectancy, and the sun struck

The water surface like a brassy palm,

Flat and gonglike, and the wave face formed.

Yes. But that was a summer so removed

In time, so specially peculiar to my life,

Why would I want to write about it again?

There was a day or two when, paddling out,

An older boy who had just graduated

And grown a great blond moustache, like a walrus,

Skimmed past me like a smooth machine on the water,

And said my name. I was so much younger,

To be identified by one like him—

The easy deference of a kind of god

Who also went to church where I did—made me

Reconsider my worth. I had been noticed.

He soon was a small figure crossing waves,

The shawling crest surrounding him with spray,

Whiter than gull feathers. He had said my name

Without scorn, just with a bit of surprise

To notice me among those trying the big waves

Of the morning break. His name is carved now

On the black wall in Washington, the frozen wave

That grievers cross to find a name or names.

I knew him as I say I knew him, then,

Which wasn't very well. My father preached

His funeral. He came home in a bag

That may have mixed in pieces of his squad.

Yes, I can write about a lot of things

Besides the summer that I turned sixteen.

But that's my ground swell. I must start

Where things began to happen and I knew it.

Transfiguration

And there appeared to them Elijah and Moses and they were talking to Jesus.
Mark 9:2

1

They were talking to him about resurrection, about law, about the
    suffering ahead.
They were talking as if to remind him who he was and who they were.
    He was not
Like his three friends watching a little way off, not like the crowd
At the foot of the hill. A gray-green thunderhead massed from the sea
And God spoke from it and said he was his. They were talking
About how the body, broken or burned, could live again, remade.
Only the fiery text of the thunderhead could explain it. And they were
    talking
About pain and the need for judgment and how he would make himself
A law of pain, both its spirit and its letter in his own flesh, and then
    break it,
That is, transcend it. His clothes flared like magnesium, as they talked.

2

When we brought our mother to him, we said, "Lord, she falls down
    the stairs.
She cannot hold her water. In the afternoon she forgets the morning."
And he said, "All things are possible to those who believe. Shave her
    head,

Insert a silicone tube inside her skull, and run it under her scalp,

Down her neck, and over her collarbone, and lead it into her stomach."

And we did and saw that she no longer stumbled or wet herself.

She could remember the morning until the evening came. And we went
    our way,

Rejoicing as much as we could, for we had worried many years.

3

They were talking to him about heaven, how all forms there were
    luciform,

How the leather girdle and the matted hair, how the lice coursing the
    skin

And the skin skinned alive, blaze with perfection, the vibrance of light.

And they were talking about the complexities of blood and lymph,

Each component crowding the vessels, the body and the antibody,

And they were talking about the lamp burning in the skull's niche,

The eyes drinking light from within and light from without,

And how simple it is to see the future, if you looked at it like the past,

And how the present belonged to the flesh and its density and darkness

And was hard to talk about. Before and after were easier. They talked
    about light.

4

A man came to him who said he had been blind since his wedding day

And had never seen his wife under the veil or the children she had

    given him.

And the Lord said, "Tell me about your parents." And the man talked

A long time, remembering how his mother cut his father's meat at

    dinner,

And how at night their voices crept along his bedroom ceiling, like—

But he could not say what they were like. And in the morning,

    everything began to tick

And ticked all day as if . . . Now, he remembered!

And suddenly his sight came back and blinded him, like a flashbulb.

5

They were talking to him about law and how lawgiving should be

Like rainfall, a light rain falling all morning and mixing with dew—

A rain that passes through the spider web and penetrates the dirt clod

Without melting it, a persistent, suffusing shower, soaking clothes,

Making sweatshirts heavier, wool stink, and finding every hair's root on

    the scalp.

And that is when you hurled judgment into the crowd and watched

    them

Spook like cattle, reached in and stirred the turmoil faster, scarier.

And they were saying that, to save the best, many must be punished,

Including the best. And no one was exempt, as they explained it,

Not themselves, not him, or anyone he loved, anyone who loved him.

6

Take anyone and plant a change inside them that they feel

And send them to an authority to assess that feeling. When they are

    told

That for them alone there waits a suffering in accordance with the laws

Of their condition, from which they may recover or may not,

Then they know the vortex on the mountaintop, the inside of the

    unspeakable,

The speechlessness before the voices begin talking to them,

Talking to prepare them, arm them and disarm them, until the end.

And if anybody's looking, they will seem transfigured.

7

I want to believe that he talked back to them, his radiant companions,

And I want to believe he said too much was being asked and too much

    promised.

I want to believe that that was why he shone in the eyes of his friends,

The witnesses looking on, because he spoke for them, because he loved
them

And was embarrassed to learn how he and they were going to suffer.

I want to believe he resisted at that moment, when he appeared
glorified,

Because he could not reconcile the contradictions and suspected

That love had a finite span and was merely the comfort of the lost.

I know he must have acceded to his duty, but I want to believe

He was transfigured by resistance, as he listened, and they talked.

Proverbs

Three things are too wonderful for me;
Four I do not understand:
The way of an eagle in the sky,
The way of a serpent on a rock,
The way of a ship on the high seas,
And the way of a man with a maiden.
Proverbs 30: 18–19

Three things are too wonderful for me;

    Four I do not understand;

Five fill me with awe; six I love:

    Our souls awake; our bodies awake;

The envelope of our tension;

    The arcing cry of release;

The silence of the house at night;

    The deep sleep of our children.

Three things are too wonderful for me—

    Four I do not understand:

The child fading in the face bones;

    Appetite and failure

Becoming distinct in the face;

    Aging, its lightness and heaviness,

Floating away, sinking;

    And the inner solitude,

The hermit brain, the heart like a recluse.

∞

Most primitive, most original, first,
     As blind with ego as a baby's fist,
The heart takes hold of speech,
     It takes and holds the word *heart*
And the thought, making both feel
     Their own pulse, their heart's life.

Three things wake me in the night—
     Four things at 3 a.m.:
Her absence from my side;
     The ceiling of time like an eyelid;
A child talking in sleep;
     The close knocking of a narrow space.

Three things erase the future—
     Four make the past a dream:
The entrance of God into history;
     The knowledge that now he is caught;
The temporary perfection

Of lovers fitting together,

Going on and on for a moment;

And the memory of that moment.

This is the way with daily life—

From waking to sleeping is like this:

Morning rising lighter than air,

And at midday, a shift, a tilting;

Then, the descent through clouds;

The desire for another body;

And foundation again, weight

Of the earth, the earth's core.

Three things are too wonderful for me—

Four I do not understand:

The aching fabric of desire;

The firmness, head to foot,

Of the absent one you need;

The light her body is made of;

The gravity of light.

∞

Three things name God—

    Four establish God's presence:

The inner voice saying *Live*;

    The outer voice saying *Live*;

The voice saying, "Oh, my God!"

    At the abrupt stoppage of time;

And repeating, like a psalm,

    "My whole body is moving."

Dressing My Daughters

One girl a full head taller

Than the other—into their Sunday dresses.

First, the slip, hardly a piece of fabric,

Softly stitched and printed with a bud.

I'm not their mother, and tangle, then untangle

The whole cloth—on backward, have to grab it

Round their necks. But they know how to pull

Arms in, a reflex of being dressed,

And also, a child's faith. The mass of stuff

That makes the Sunday frocks collapses

In my hands and finds its shape, only because

They understand the drape of it

These skinny keys to intricate locks.

The buttons are a problem

For a surgeon. How would she connect

These bony valves and stubborn eyelets?

The filmy dress revolves in my blind fingers.

The slots work one by one.

And when they're put together,

Not like puppets or those doll-saints

That bring tears to true believers,

But living children, somebody's real daughters,

They do become more real.

They say, "Stop it!" and "Give it back!"

And "I don't want to!" They'll kiss

A doll's hard features, whispering,

"I'm sorry." I know just why my mother

Used to worry. Your clothes don't keep

You close—it's nakedness.

Clad in my boots and holster,

I would roam with my six-gun buddies.

We dealt fake death to one another,

Fell and rolled in filth and rose,

Grimy with wounds, then headed home.

But Sunday. . . . What was that tired explanation

Given for wearing clothes that

Scratched and shone and weighed like a slow hour?

That we should shine—in gratitude.

So, I give that explanation, undressing them,

And wait for the result.

After a day like Sunday, such a long one,

When they lie down, half-dead,

To be undone, they won't help me.

They cry, "It's not my fault."

After Disappointment

To lie in your child's bed when she is gone
Is calming as anything I know. To fall
Asleep, her books arranged above your head,
Is to admit that you have never been
So tired, so enchanted by the spell
Of your grown body. To feel small instead
Of blocking out the light, to feel alone,
Not knowing what you should or shouldn't feel,
Is to find out, no matter what you've said
About the cramped escapes and obstacles
You plan and face and have to call the world,
That there remain these places, occupied
By children, yours if lucky, like the girl
Who finds you here and lies down by your side.

Wave

Always offshore, or already broken, gone;
Foaming around the skin;
Its print embedded in the rigid sand;
Rising from almost nothing on the beach
To show its brood of gravel,
Then coming down hard, making its point felt.

Saying, "This time I mean it. This time I will
Not have to do it over;"
Repeating as if to perfect, as if,
Repeated, each were perfect; all forgotten,
One by one by one;
Every one, monster or beauty, going smash.

Wall after falling wall out to the sunset;
Or the ugly freak, capsizing
The fishing boat, reforming, riding on;
Still beautiful, lifting the frond of kelp,
Holding the silversides
Up to the eye, coming ashore in dreams.

∞

Coming to light; invisible, appearing

To be the skeleton

Of water, or its muscle, or the look

Crossing its face; intelligence or instinct

Or neither; all we see

In substance moving toward us, all we wish for.

Already rising, lump in the throat, pulse

That taps the fingertip;

The word made flesh, gooseflesh; placid, the skin,

Remembering the sudden agitation,

Swelling again with pleasure;

All riders lifted easily as light.

Grid

I walk those streets tonight, streets named for gems,

And streets that cross them named for Spanish women.

The gem streets end at the ocean, looking out.

Each woman wears a string of them and ends

With nothing on the edge of town. They are

Juanita, Inez, Maria, Lucia, Elena.

Their jewels are Opal, Emerald, Carnelian,

Topaz, Sapphire, Pearl, Ruby, Diamond.

I'm never sure I've named them all or walked

Along them all. Some are like boulevards.

Those are the gem streets. Some little more than lanes—

Those are the women. Yet I have searched for Opal

Among dead ends and alleys and discovered it

Dangling from Maria's wrist, or Juanita's.

All the life I care about, or almost all,

Lived first along these streets. That life is gone.

And when I say, "I walk those streets tonight,"

It's only poetry. I, too, am gone.

The streets maintain their urban grid, their limits.

The gem streets end at the ocean, the blank Pacific.

And the ones that wear them, named for Spanish women,

Themselves end on the edge of town with nothing.

Questions for Ecclesiastes

What if on a foggy night in a beachtown, a night when the Pacific
leans close like the face of a wet cliff, a preacher were called to
the house of a suicide, a house of strangers, where a child had
discharged a rifle through the roof of her mouth and the top of
her skull?

What if he went to the house where the parents, stunned into plaster
statues, sat behind their coffee table, and what if he assured
them that the sun would rise and go down, the wind blow south,
then turn north, whirling constantly, rivers—even the concrete
flume of the great Los Angeles—run into the sea, and fourteen-
year-old girls would manage to spirit themselves out of life,
nothing was new under the sun?

What if he said the eye is not satisfied with seeing, nor the ear filled
with hearing? Would he want to view the bedroom vandalized
by self-murder or hear the quiet before the tremendous shout of
the gun or the people inside the shout, shouting or screaming,
crying and pounding to get into the room, kicking through the
hollow core door and making a new sound and becoming a new
silence—the silence he entered with his comfort?

∞

What if as comfort he said to the survivors, I praise the dead which
are dead already more than the living, and better is he than both
dead and living who is not yet alive? What if he folded his hands
together and ate his own flesh in prayer? For he did pray with
them. He asked them, the mother and father, if they wished to
pray to do so in any way they felt comfortable, and the father
knelt at the coffee table and the mother turned to squeeze her
eyes into a corner of the couch, and they prayed by first listening
to his prayer, then clawing at his measured cadences with
tears (the man cried) and curses (the woman swore). What if,
then, the preacher said be not rash with thy mouth and let not
thine heart be hasty to utter anything before God: for God is in
heaven?

What if the parents collected themselves, then, and asked him
to follow them to their daughter's room, and stood at the
shattered door, the darkness of the room beyond, and the
father reached in to put his hand on the light switch and asked
if the comforter, the preacher they were meeting for the first
time in their lives, would like to see the aftermath, and instead
of recoiling and apologizing, he said that the dead know not

anything for the memory of them is forgotten? And while standing in the hallway, he noticed the shag carpet underfoot, like the fur of a cartoon animal, the sort that requires combing with a plastic rake, leading into the bedroom, where it would have to be taken up, skinned off the concrete slab of the floor, and still he said for their love and hatred and envy are now perished, neither have the dead any more portion for ever in anything that is done under the sun?

What if as an act of mercy so acute it pierced the preacher's skull and traveled the length of his spine, the man did not make him regard the memory of his daughter as it must have filled her room, but guided the wise man, the comforter, to the front door, with his wife with her arms crossed before her in that gesture we use to show a stranger to the door, acting out a rite of closure, compelled to be social, as we try to extricate ourselves by breaking off the extensions of our bodies, as raccoons gnaw their legs from traps, turning aside our gaze, letting only the numb tissue of valedictory speech ease us apart, and the preacher said live joyfully all the days of the life of thy vanity, for that is thy portion in this life?

They all seem worse than heartless, don't they, these crass and
irrelevant platitudes, albeit stoical and final, oracular, stony, and
comfortless? But they were at the center of that night, even if
they were unspoken.

And what if one with only a casual connection to the tragedy
remembers a man, younger than I am today, going out after
dinner and returning, then sitting in the living room, drinking a
cup of tea, slowly finding the strength to say he had visited these
grieving strangers and spent some time with them?

Still that night exists for people I do not know in ways I do not
know, though I have tried to imagine them. I remember my
father going out and my father coming back. The fog, like the
underskin of a broken wave, made a low ceiling that the street
lights pierced and illuminated. And God who shall bring every
work into judgment, with every secret thing, whether it be good
or whether it be evil, who could have shared what He knew with
people who needed urgently to hear it, God kept a secret.

Upwelling

Under the wave, the gray, clamping pressure—

Strange, in that moment, to remember, posed
Beside a pavement sapling with a girl
Who feared and loved him, Kevin Horrigan,
His face like a manhole cover, his crime coming
With a tire iron clanging on a can lid,
Still wanting, in that moment, something nice.

Under tons of foam, palms pressed, chest down on sand—

And still to wonder how a kiss would taste,
If only she would come down here and press
Her body close, but with a softer pressure.
Passing a word between her lips, into
A cloud of longing, she kisses air goodbye.
Felicia Smith—she kisses air goodbye.

Eyes stung, breath held in the down-rush, then—

To know the heart of Johnny Lopez, suddenly
Changed overnight from boy to brooding man,

No way to bring him back, coiling laughter

Around and round his fist like a wet rag,

The laughter of boys,—to know his coiled heart,

To feel it, and the sudden end of childhood,

Like bringing down the house to shut a suitcase.

And now the morning wells up from a dream,

A face lies close, and there are children waking,

Like echoes, in another room. The past

Folds back into the past, and out of sleep,

The streaming peace below the wave, you come

(You . . . you. Who *are* you?)—

Suspended, like a sentence, in the present.

Unholy Sonnets

1

Dear God, Our Heavenly Father, Gracious Lord,
Mother Love and Maker, Light Divine,
Atomic Fingertip, Cosmic Design,
First Letter of the Alphabet, Last Word,
Mutual Satisfaction, Cash Award,
Auditor Who Approves Our Bottom Line,
Examiner Who Says That We Are Fine,
Oasis That All Sands Are Running Toward.

I can say almost anything about you,
O Big Idea, and with each epithet,
Create new reasons to believe or doubt you,
Black Hole, White Hole, Presidential Jet.
But what's the anything I must leave out? You
Solve nothing but the problems that I set.

2

Hands folded to construct a church and steeple,
A roof of knuckles, outer walls of skin,
The thumbs as doors, the fingers bent within
To be revealed, wriggling, as "all the people,"
All eight of them, enmeshed, caught by surprise,
Turned upward blushing in the sudden light,
The nails like welders' masks, the fit so tight
Among them you can hear their half-choked cries
To be released, to be pried from this mess
They're soldered into somehow—they don't know.
But stuck now they are willing to confess,
If that will ease your grip and let them go,
Confess the terror they cannot withstand
Is being locked inside another hand.

3

Balaam upon his ass was unaware
That he was not completely in control
Or that his own ego was not his soul.
His ass, however, knew enough to fear
The figure standing in the thoroughfare.
God opened the ass's mouth so she could tell
Balaam, who could not see the obstacle,
That striking her, as he had, was unfair.

I want like Balaam to be shown my soul.
His was a donkey blessed with second sight,
Endowed with speech to limn the invisible.
And mine—will it rear up in holy fright
Or stall before the garage doors of hell?
I need a metaphor to sleep tonight.

4

Amazing to believe that nothingness
Surrounds us with delight and lets us be,
And that the meekness of nonentity,
Despite the friction of the world of sense,
Despite the leveling of violence,
Is all that matters. All the energy
We force into the matchhead and the city
Explodes inside a loving emptiness.

Not Dante's rings, not the Zen zero's mouth,
Out of which comes and into which light goes,
This God recedes from every metaphor,
Turns the hardest data into untruth,
And fills all blanks with blankness. This love shows
Itself in absence, which the stars adore.

5

This is the moment. This is all we have.
But how can we say this? What do we mean
By saying this to children, like sad men
With minds gone rotten in a sexual hive,
Who show children the secret thing they have—
The answer to all questions? What do we mean,
Then, by the souls of children, women, men?
The question stung and swollen in the hive.
I think I know sometimes and feel the joy
Of loving only for a lifetime. Death
Will smoke us out like bees, but we'll forget
That we were going to see the end of joy.
Our souls will keep like honey after death.
We'll forget that we were going to forget.

6

Look into the darkness and the darkness looks—
As if it massed before a telescope
Or turned because behind it heard your step—
The darkness looks at you. This idea spooks
Some people, and their reason self-destructs.
Seized by a love of daylight, back they jump
Into the known, blazing like a headlamp,
Into the senses tuned like cars and trucks.

And what about the counsel of my friend
Who says that when we look for God, remember
God looks for us? If that's what starts the thing,
Then we must drive in circles till we find
It's all one. To be looked for is to look for.
And seeing is believing and being seen.

7

Reduce the proof of nature. So we tried

And still found that our bodies kept their faith.

Reduce the body, burn away the brain.

We tried and found the chemical debris

Inscribed with calculations of a mind.

Reduce the compounds, elements, all bits

Of matter, energy. Make all abstract.

We tried and met the idea of the act.

But what was that? Without prerequisites

Of . . . You know what I mean. We couldn't find . . .

What's the word for it? We couldn't see . . .

But any metaphor will seem inane.

Without the world, we met the death

Of God. And language. Both of them had died.

8

Two forces rule the universe of breath
And one is gravity and one is light.
And does their jurisdiction include death?
Does nothingness exist in its own right?
It's hard to say, lying awake at night,
Full of an inner weight, a glaring dread,
And feeling that Simone Weil must be right.
Two forces rule the universe, she said,
And they are light and gravity. And dead,
She knows, as you and I do not, if death
Is also ruled or if it rules instead,
And if it matters, after your last breath.
But she said truth was on the side of death
And thought God's grace filled emptiness, like breath.

9

Almighty God, to you all hearts are open,

All throats, all voice boxes, all inner ears,

All pupils, all tear ducts, all cavities

Inside the skull inside the trick of flesh.

To you the face is like a picture window,

The body is a door of molded glass,

All lengths of gut are pasture, all membrane

Peels back and off like ripe persimmon skin.

And every wrinkle folded in the brain

Runs smoothly through your fingers and snaps back

Into its convolution. Even the blood

Is naked as a bolt of oilcloth.

You touch the working parts and track the thought,

A comet on your fingertip, and squint.

10

Time to admit my altar is a desk.
Time to confess the cross I bear a pen.
My soul, a little like a compact disc,
Slides into place, a laser plays upon
Its surface, and a sentimental mist,
Freaked with the colors of church window glass,
Rides down a shaft of light that smells of must
As music adds a layer of high gloss.
Time to say plainly when I am alone
And waiting for the coming of the ghost
Whose flame-tongue like a blow torch, sharp and lean,
Writes things that no one ever could have guessed,
I give in to my habit and my vice
And speak as soon as I can find a voice.

11

Half asleep in prayer I said the right thing
And felt a sudden pleasure come into
The room or my own body. In the dark,
Charged with a change of atmosphere, at first
I couldn't tell my body from the room.
And I was wide awake, full of this feeling,
Alert as though I'd heard a doorknob twist,
A drawer pulled, and instead of terror knew
The intrusion of an overwhelming joy.
I had said thanks and this was the response.
But how I said it or what I said it for
I still cannot recall and I have tried
All sorts of ways all hours of the night.
Once was enough to be dissatisfied.

12

There was a pious man upright as Job,

In fact, more pious, more upright, who prayed

The way most people thoughtlessly enjoy

Their stream of consciousness. He concentrated

On glorifying God, as some men let

Their minds create and fondle curving shadows.

And as he gained in bumper crops and cattle,

He greeted each success with grave amens.

So he was shocked, returning from the bank,

To see a flood bearing his farm away—

His cows, his kids, his wife, and all his stuff.

Swept off his feet, he cried out, "Why?" and sank.

And God grumped from his rain cloud, "I can't say.

Just something about you pisses me off."

13

Drunk on the Umbrian hills at dusk and drunk
On one pink cloud that stood beside the moon,
Drunk on the moon, a marble smile, and drunk,
Two young Americans, on one another,
Far from home and wanting this forever—
Who needed God? We had our bodies, bread,
And glasses of a raw, green, local wine,
And watched our Godless perfect darkness breed
Enormous softly burning ancient stars.
Who needed God? And why do I ask now?
Because I'm older and I think God stirs
In details that keep bringing back that time,
Details that are just as vivid now—
Our bodies, bread, a sharp Umbrian wine.

14

After the praying, after the hymn-singing,
After the sermon's trenchant commentary
On the world's ills, which make ours secondary,
After communion, after the hand-wringing,
And after peace descends upon us, bringing
Our eyes up to regard the sanctuary
And how the light swords through it, and how, scary
In their sheer numbers, motes of dust ride, clinging—
There is, as doctors say about some pain,
Discomfort knowing that despite your prayers,
Your listening and rejoicing, your small part
In this communal stab at coming clean,
There is one stubborn remnant of your cares
Intact. There is still murder in your heart.

15

A useful God will roost in a bird-box,
Wedge-head thrust out, red-feathered in the sun,
Each huge eye squinting through a minus sign,
His stiffened wakefulness, like a bird book's
Audubon print, hiding his claws' and beak's
Readiness to enjoy their work and soon.
A God like that will watch us think of sin,
Tilting his head, before he shrugs and backs
Away inside, leaving an empty hole.
Something of nature for the neighborhood,
Charming in daylight, while the pose is held . . .
We know, of course, in darkness rats are harried,
Moles are dismembered, and their screams are horrid.
A God like that can make the nighttime hell.

16

We drove to the world's end and there betrayed

The ones we promised not to. While we drove

We talked about the afterlife and love,

Slowing to an impatient crawl, delayed

By roadwork, in an idling parade

We couldn't see the head or tail of.

We inched past miles of asphalt, reeking stuff,

Stroked by a rake of fire as it was laid.

And we agreed the analogues for hell

Came to us everywhere we looked in life.

But not for heaven. For it we couldn't find

A metaphor or likeness. Not until

We had betrayed our loved ones, at the end,

Did we have something to compare it with.

17

God like a kiss, God like a welcoming,

God like a hand guiding another hand

And raising it or making it descend,

God like the pulse point and its silent drumming,

And the tongue going to it, God like the humming

Of pleasure if the skin felt it as sound,

God like the hidden wanting to be found

And like the joy of being and becoming.

And God the understood, the understanding,

And God the pressure trying to relieve

What is not pain but names itself with weeping,

And God the rush of time and God time standing,

And God the touch body and soul believe,

And God the secret neither one is keeping.

18

In *Civilization and Its Discontents*
Freud quotes the poet Heine in a footnote
That's *Schadenfreude* incarnate. Heine wrote
(Although I'm playing loosely with the sense):
"My needs are few and my desires but these—
A woodland house, the best of simple food,
And just outside my door, if God is good,
Some six or seven of my enemies,
Strung up so as to make my heart swell full.
Before they died, I would forgive them all
The wrongs they'd done me—grant them absolution.
For to do on earth as it is done in heaven,
I know one's enemies must be forgiven,
But not before they're brought to execution."

19

I swat him in the face and hope that nothing
Comes of it. Then much later, late at night,
Lying in my oblong of insomnia,
Ask for forgiveness in the form of sleep.
I hope that nothing will arouse him further,
That nothing will hurt him further, but I know,
At the top of the fenced walkway, he is waiting,
An offended fifteen-year-old with a man's fists
That come at me like bulletins, like headlines.
I will not sleep tonight. I will not sleep.
God can be hurt, the vast is vulnerable,
The infinite capacity to love can weep,
Then turn away, the dark side of the sun,
Discovered at the moment you are lost.

20

If God survives us, will his kingdom come?
But let's row out to sea and ship the oars
And watch the planet drown in meteors.
If God forgives us, surely he will come.
Can we nail up a man and do the same
To a child? Yes. And drive the spikes through tears.
But let's row out to sea and watch the stars.
No matter what we do, they are the same,
Crossing the bleeding sky on shining feet,
Walking on water toward us, and then sinking.
Surely when he grew up, God must have known
What sort of death was waiting for one thinking
That with his coming history was complete.
We'll greet him as the children would have done.

Skin Cancer

Balmy overcast nights of late-September;

Palms standing out in street light, house light;

Full moon penetrating the cloud film

With an explosive halo, a ring almost half the sky;

Air like a towel draped over shoulders;

Lightness or gravity deferred like a moral question;

The incense in the house lit; the young people

Moving from the front door into the half dark

And back, or up the stairs to glimpse the lovers' shoes

Outside the master bedroom; the youngest speculating;

The taste of beer, familiar as salt water;

Each window holding a sea view, charcoal

With shifting bars of white; the fog filling in

Like the haze of distance itself, pushing close, blurring.

As if the passage into life were through such houses,

Surrounded by some version of ocean weather,

Lit beads of fog or wind so stripped it burns the throat;

Mildew-spreading, spray-laden breezes and the beach sun

Making each grain of stucco cast a shadow;

An ideal landscape sheared of its nostalgia;

S. with his black hair, buck teeth, unsunned skin,

Joking and disappearing; F. doing exactly the same

But dying, a corkscrew motion through green water;

And C. not looking back from the car door,

Reappearing beside the East River, rich, owned, smiling at last.

Swains and nymphs. And news that came with the sea damp,

Of steady pipe-corrosions, black corners,

Moisture working through sand lots, through slab floors,

Slowly, with chemical, with molecular intricacy,

Then, bursting alive: the shrieked confessions

Of the wild parents; the cliff collapse; the kidnap;

The cache of photos; the letter; the weapon; the haunted dream;

The sudden close-up of the loved one's degradation.

Weather a part of it all, permeating and sanctifying,

Infiltrating and destroying; the sun disc,

Cool behind the veil of afternoon cloud,

With sun spots like flies crawling across it;

The slow empurpling of skin all summer;

The glorious learned flesh and the rich pallor

Of the untouched places in the first nakedness;

The working of the lesion now in late life,

Soon to be known by the body, even the one

Enduring the bareness of the inland plains,

The cold fronts out of Canada, a sickness

For home that feels no different from health.

Last Suppers

Loneliest when hung in a church annex,
Like a No Smoking sign, itself ablaze.
In the faithful reproductions the deterioration
Hangs like religious haze in the Upper Room.

Times I have noticed it was present fix
And obliterate the rooms where it was hung.
The scene so intimate in its dismay,
Familiar as a family's daily warfare.

What has happened? It's as if dinner has ended
With Father drunk again and Mother silent.
The daughters are enlisted to clean up.
They leave. And the sons begin to fight.

But, no. Christ has forecast his betrayal.
The group gesticulates, the traitor shrinks,
Spilling the salt for bad luck. And the meal
Is not finished, still has to be eaten.

•

I knew a family who hung a Last Supper

Above their dining table. A box of glass,
Like an aquarium of fish and weed,
With a lightbulb to turn the colors on.

I don't have to picture them together.
I've sat in their bitter circle, underneath
The lit-up masterpiece, heartsick, knowing
Dessert was the old man's fist against his eldest

And down the punching order to my friend.
Septic with unshed tears, he would turn on me,
And yet not bring himself to raise his fist.
His younger sister would stand up on a chair,

As Jesus and his apostles were switched off,
And point and say, "That's God." You had to answer
Before the scene went dark. You had to say,
"Yes," to her catechism. "That is God."

•

A child, I was brought into a room,
Geometrical with shadows, in Milan,

And a chill like an embrace from underground.
Our silence was a reverence for a picture.

There was the great painting behind a rope
And a parental awe I couldn't share.
I was impressed by the museum photograph
Of the bombed church and the story of survival.

The copy that we bought was done on silk.
As precious as a prayer shawl, it would hang
Beside my father's desk at church, its colors
Ancient in the fluorescent, humming light.

Alone once, going through his desk, I found
Capsules of ammonia in silk sacks,
Aids for someone who dealt with the poor in spirit,
Cracked one, and felt my head snap back.

•

The irony and genius of the thing
Is that it does not look at us. The foreground

Figures are obsessed with one another.
A landscape watches them through distant windows.

Everywhere it appears, in books, in rooms,
The painting turns it subjects toward their Lord
And one another. Their gestures sing a hymn
Of self-importance. And he averts his eyes.

On our side, the world runs through its days
Or, if you wish, it braids in endless spirals.
And what we occupy or set in motion
Jars or meshes. When we pause to look outside,

Pictures look back at us and words respond,
Images return our human gaze.
But this, despite the copying, resists.
What matters is the loneliness of God.

•

Everyone knows the silence like a wind
You have to crouch in to eat your food in safety,

Or the outburst that rains poison on the supper,
Or dining alone, in your room or with a book.

Mother coming to the table piping hot
And Father on the rocks cranky with bourbon.
The children sensing the collision coming,
Sullen themselves, urging it to happen.

The reaction could as easily take place
While getting in the car or getting out,
Around the Christmas tree or television.
All it needs is a family's critical mass.

And yet the table is a raft to cling to.
Becalmed, each pins down an unsteady edge.
And when the swell, anger, rolls through the meal,
The inner cry is "Save yourself, if you can!"

•

I have a memory of Passover,
Crackling with an air of irritation.

We feared Elijah would enrage the host,
If he appeared at all, by being late.

To put our figures back into that evening,
The young couples, the parents, the empty chair,
Risks the restorer's bungling that can hasten
Collapse. Better to say, "We ate together."

And not that one kept looking at his plate.
One drank several glasses of sweet wine.
There was a moment nobody would speak.
Two fell out of love across the table.

Now the scene only retains its lines.
Color and character—the eyes, for example—
Are lost in clouds of crumbled memory.
Whole areas—the room, the year—have vanished.

●

The tumult of the twelve thrusts out a snaking
Embrace to clutch us close and feel the pressure

Of our belief or nonbelief. It pulls,
In either case, the eye close to the faces.

And most of them are marred beyond belief.
They fade in the pointillism of decay,
Like blown-up newspaper photography.
What moves us in the remnants? Common pathos.

Leonardo set the catastrophe in motion
By giving himself time to work slowly,
Thus mixed a base that let him perfect details.
In making the picture right he made it mortal.

Most copies restore exact lines and colors,
Unsubtly, like parade floats or modern
Translations of translations of the Bible.
But the crudest replica can smell of blood.

•

In the original the decay is like a smoke cloud,
Materializing from the walls and ceiling.

Someone, by now, should have called out, "Fire!"
And someone has, the calm one, at the center.

He has said it sadly, "Fire," and those hearing
Confer among themselves and make petitions
To ascertain if the announcement's really true.
Looked at thus they look ridiculous.

But as the smoke clears, they're not what I see,
Seized in their poses by a passion's heat.
I see a family's uninspired tableau,
Touched for once by a deep tranquillity.

They link hands, close eyes, pass a loving pressure,
Safe from disasters only God and Art
Would call down on their heads. When their eyes open,
They eat and drink and talk, at ease, in peace.

The Worry Bird

God was an idea before God was an image.

And yet there are things like the worry bird

That stay with us through life and intercede

With an old darkness, filling an old need.

Hunched on a plaster base, a buffoon buzzard,

Like a firesale souvenir or piece of flood damage,

With a ruff of blue duck-down, and a rubber beak

Like a gray sock between its hang-dog eyes,

It stood beseechingly at the bedside.

"Don't be silly," they told us when we cried,

"Give your worries to the worry bird." Its gaze,

A weary martyr's, listened to us speak

As we learned patiently to say our prayers

That also left us lying in the dark,

Fringed with the light seeping under a door.

Though childhood turns abstract as we get older,

The worry bird remains, with its wry look

And slumped wing shoulders, sagging with old cares:

The half hour they were late home from their party,

The lies told at school, accumulating,

The broken heirloom hidden in a drawer,

All things we don't think much of anymore,

Replaced by the grown world's escalating

Nightmares about career, money, duty.

The worry bird was meant to make us smile

As they smiled at our miniature infernos.

We know now they were right. And in their beds,

As we now know since we've seen inside their heads,

They had no silly icon for their troubles,—

Only an idea, if at all. Meanwhile,

The worry bird takes on another form

And watches with another shade of interest,

Circling among the other distant images

That used to help and still do. Mirages

Of comfort, they can bring a kind of rest

Anyone who has been a child can know.

Unholy Sonnets (2000)

Prologue

Please be the driver bearing down behind,
Or swerve in front and slow down to a crawl,
Or leave a space to lure me in, then pull
Ahead, cutting me off, and blast your horn.
Please climb the mountain with me, tailgating
And trying to overtake on straightaways.
Let nightfall make us both pick up the pace,
Trading positions with our high beams glaring.
And when we have exhausted sanity
And fuel, and smoked our engines, then, please stop,
Lurching onto the shoulder of the road,
And get out, raging, and walk up to me,
Giving me time to feel my stomach drop,
And see you face to face, and say, "My Lord!"

The Word "Answer"

Prayer exerts an influence upon God's action, even upon his existence. This is what the word "answer" means. —Karl Barth, *Prayer*

Lightning walks across the shallow seas,

Stick figures putting feet down hard

Among the molecules. Meteors dissolve

And drop their pieces in a mist of iron,

Drunk through atomic skin like dreamy wine.

The virus that would turn a leaf dark red

Seizes two others that would keep it green.

They spread four fingers like a lizard's hand.

Into this random rightness comes the prayer,

A change of weather, a small shift of degree

That heaves a desert where a forest sweated,

And asks creation to return an answer.

That's all it wants: a prayer just wants an answer,

And twists time in a knot until it gets it.

There's the door. Will anybody get it?

That's what he's wondering; the bath's still warm;

And by the time he towels off and puts on

His pajamas, robe, and slippers and goes down,

They'll be gone, won't they? There's the door again;

And nobody's here to answer it but him.

Perhaps they'll go away. But it's not easy,

Relaxing in the tub, reading the paper,

With someone at the front door, ringing and pounding,

And—that sounds like glass—breaking in.

At least the bathroom door's securely bolted.

Or is that any assurance in this case?

He might as well go find out what's the matter.

Whoever it is must really want . . . something.

We ask for bread, he makes his body bread.

We ask for daily life, and every day,

We get a life, or a facsimile,

Or else we get a tight place in a crowd

Or test results with the prognosis—bad.

We ask and what is given is the answer,

For we can always see it as an answer,

Distorted as it may be, from our God.

What shall we ask for then? For his return,

Like the bereaved parents with the monkey's paw,

Wishing, then wishing again? The last answer,

When we have asked for all that we can ask for,

May be the end of time, our mangled child,
And in the doorway, dead, the risen past.

With this prayer I am making up a God
On a gray day, prophesying snow.
I pray that God be immanent as snow
When it has fallen deeply, a deep God.
With this prayer I am making up a God
Who answers prayer, responding like the snow
To footprints and the wind, to a child in snow
Making an angel who will speak for God.
God, I am thinking of you now as snow,
Descending like the answer to a prayer,
This prayer that you will be made visible,
Drifting and deepening, a dazzling, slow
Acknowledgement, out of the freezing air,
As dangerous as it is beautiful.

Someone Is Always Praying

Someone is always praying as the plane

Breaks up, and smoke and cold and darkness blow

Into the cabin. Praying as it happens,

Praying before it happens that it won't.

Someone was praying that it never happen

Before the first window on Kristallnacht

Broke like a wine glass wrapped in bridal linen.

Before it was imagined, someone was praying

That it be unimaginable. And then,

The bolts blew off and people fell like bombs

Out of their names, out of the living sky.

Surely, someone was praying. And the prayer

Struck the blank face of earth, the ocean's face,

The rockhard, rippled face of facelessness.

Cycle

Everything around the central meaning,
Whatever grips that something in the womb
And, when a door slams, looks as if it's leaning
From all the objects in a startled room;
Everything that passes through the puzzle
A spider glues together or is caught,
And bends the whisker back until the muzzle
Twitches, and tugs, then loosens the square knot;
Everything surrounding everything
That's going to happen, even the manger's planks,
The barn's stone lintels, poised as if to sing,
The angel choir of matter giving thanks;
And all that made the world seem passing strange:
Everything is about to know a change.

Everything is about to know a change,
For someone will appear and say a word,
And someone else will hear and rearrange
His life as no one ever thought he would.
And something like an earthquake or a storm
Will happen somewhere like a little town,
And that place, although nothing but a stem,

Will snap off and the tree will tumble down.

And the about-to-be, a secret cache,

Will smoulder like a spark inside a couch,

And those who sat in darkness, dropping ash,

Will see a great light. Everyone will touch

And be touched by the change no one can stop.

A single leaf will speak. A voice will drop.

A voice will speak. A single leaf will drop.

And the whole tree will wither where it stands

And never bear again, though he could help,

As he has helped the withered bones of hands,

The corneas of clouded over eyes,

The blood and breath of loved ones, dead and dying,

And even water, calming frantic seas,

And even water, turning it to wine.

The poor world must have fallen with the fall

For him to curse a fruit tree, out of season,

For giving nothing, like an unborn apple,

And then to make up, for some obscure reason,

A lesson on the power of faith and prayer.

Perhaps to understand, you had to be there.

∞

Perhaps to understand you had to be

Alone with the absent presence he called father,

Alone with the dysfunctional family

Of stars and darkness, deaf and dumb together,

And in that interaction see a sign,

The way a bedside watcher will believe

A twitch or flicker—almost anything—

Is proof the injured sleeper will revive.

Perhaps to understand, you had to die,

Having acknowledged with your body's pain

That everybody does, unmythically,

Knowing only that it won't happen again,

And then to wake and find your death the proof

Of an abstraction that the world calls love.

The abstraction that the world calls love

Appeared to grieving friends and cooked them food

And walked with them a way and let one shove

Fingers into his wounds and take a good

Look. And then he turned to wind and fire

And pieces of his clothes and eyelashes

And thorns and rusty nails and locks of hair
And red letters on a few translucent pages.
He took on flesh and then he took it off,
Or else he kept it for a souvenir,
Or else—but why keep going back and forth?
He dwelt among us, then he disappeared.
And we are left to be and keep on being,
Like everything around a central meaning.

Breath Like a House Fly

Breath like a house fly batters the shut mouth.

The dream begins, turns over, and goes flat.

The virus cleans the attic and heads south.

Somebody asks, "What did you mean by that?"

But nobody says, "Nothing," in response.

Silence becomes the question and the answer.

The ghost abandons all of his old haunts.

The body turns a last cell into cancer.

And then—banal epiphany—and then,

Time kick starts and the deaf brain hears a voice.

The eyes like orphans find the world again.

Day washes down the city streets with noise.

And oxygen repaints the blood bright red.

How good it is to come back from the dead!

Sightings

Kenosis

An absence turned to presence is confusing.

Take Mary, who took for a gardener

One that she knew was dead and in his grave,

One that she then called Master, when he stood

Before her and said, "Mary," and resisted

Her startled, tender, human wish to touch.

We want to fill the emptiness with meaning.

I had a friend whose father died in his armchair.

And when my friend came home, there was a drape

With the body slumped beneath it, still in the chair.

She said, "I knew that must be him. And yet,

It was a shock to see him sitting there,

So present and not present, this big man,

Filling his place as much or more than ever."

Emmaus

They're eating dinner with someone they loved,

Someone almost forgotten from their past,

Who has come back. And they are all amazed

And look on as they chew, as their friend talks

And breaks a fresh loaf open, and remarks

It's *like* something, and offers it to them

And says it yields up truth like a sweet savor.

They put their noses to the fractured crust.

But it's not bread they're breathing. It is words.

And then, they are alone, thinking of things

To ask that now they can't. What's a "sweet savor"?

And all they have is right before their eyes,

Bread crumbs, some honey, and a piece of fish,

All of which tastes like joy and disbelief.

Damascus

Headlong in your career, breathing out threatening

And slaughter against enemies, dictating trouble

For anyone advanced ahead of you, gambling

That you can stay ahead of your rep, checking off

The list of those to chop off at the top, and the place

Your name will be inked in, all the while businesslike,

Congenial with associates and flattering

To authorities and enforcers, bloody and obscene

Only in private mutterings and unspoken dreams,

On your way to yet another hanging, stoning, gossip-

Mongering swap meet of assassins, you're surprised

As much as anyone to be chosen—though it requires

A certain blindness on your part and such a change

You wouldn't know yourself—a vessel of grace.

Patmos

On a clear day you can see dark matter—

And still not know what you are looking at.

Or turn and see the simple heavens shatter

And make themselves into an alphabet

Of riddles wrapped inside of mysteries

Inside enigmas, coming from deep space.

What do you do when everything's a sign

And the goatskin of the universe uncaps

And pours its missing mass out like a wine?

I saw the script that glares inside rubbed eyes.

I felt the infrastructure of the face

Which will endure though empires collapse.

I was astonished, I could hardly speak,

And wrote it all down afterward, in Greek.

Nothing But Pleasure

Nothing but pleasure in the bottle's voice

As the cork pulls from its neck. Nothing, as

The wine finds its legs in the bell of the glass,

But pleasure, on the lips, on the tongue, in the muscles

And veins of the throat. And though darkness hovers above

The candle flames, there is only pleasure when

The face flushes and the lover sees it. Only

Pleasure somehow in that redness and that witness,

As the food (some dish prepared for the pure pleasure of it)

Is consumed. Pleasure, a small god, absent

From the vast and crowded morgues of heaven and hell,

Is our true god. As the lovers disrobe and embrace

And nakedness becomes as delectable

As butter and olive oil, only pleasure watches.

The World

The world works for us and we call it grace.

It works against us and, if we are brave,

We call it nothing and we keep our faith,

And only to ourselves we call it fate.

What makes the world work? No one seems to know.

The clouds arrange the weather, the sea goes

Deep, a black stillness seethes at the earth's core,

And somebody invents the telephone.

If we are smart, we know where we fit in.

If we are lucky, we know what to bid.

If we are good, we know a charming fib

Can do more good than harm. So we tell it.

The world was meant to operate like this.

The working of the world was ever thus.

The working of the world was ever thus.

The empty air surrounds us with its love.

A fire in the skull ignites the sun.

The skin of water opens at a touch.

And earth erupts, earth curves away, earth yields.

Someone imagines strife and someone peace.

Someone inserts the god in the machine

And someone picks him out like a poppy seed.

In every new construction of desire,

The old dissatisfactions rule the eyes.

The new moon eats the old and, slice by slice,

Rebuilds a face of luminous delight,

In which we see ourselves, at last, make sense.

It is the mirror in everything that shines.

It is the mirror in everything that shines

And makes the soul the color of the sky

And clarifies and gradually blinds

And shows the spider its enormous bride.

And we show our reluctant gratitude,

Searching the paths and runways for a spoor

Of cosmic personality, one clue,

Even the fossil light of burned-out proof.

It is enough and not enough to sketch

The human mask inside the swarming nest

And hold the face, a template, to the egg

And stamp its features on the blank of death.

Although we break rock open to find life,

We cannot stare the strangeness from the leaf.

We cannot stare the strangeness from the leaf,
And so we spin all difference on a wheel
And blur it into likeness. So we seize
The firefly and teach it human need
And mine its phosphor for cold light and call
Across the world as if it were a lawn,
Blinking awake at summer dusk. We talk
Ceaselessly to things that can't respond
Or won't respond. What are we talking for?
We're talking to coax hope and love from zero.
We're talking so the brain of the geode
Will listen like a garden heliotrope
And open its quartz flowers. We are talking
Because speech is a sun, a kind of making.

Because speech is a sun, a kind of making,
And muteness we have always found estranging,
Because even our silences are phrasing
And language is the tongue we curl for naming,
Because we want the earth to be like heaven
And heaven to be everywhere we're headed,

Because we hope our formulae, like hexes,

Will stop and speed up time at our behesting,

There is no help for us, and that's our glory.

A furious refusal to acknowledge,

Except in words, the smallness of our portion,

Pumps heart, lights brain, and conjures up a soul

From next to nothing. We know all flesh is grass.

And when the world works, we still call it grace.

Epilogue

Today is fresh, and yesterday is stale.

Today is fast, and yesterday is slow.

Today is yes, and yesterday is no.

Today is news, and yesterday's a tale.

The grave is empty. Last night it was full.

The glorious means of death was once a shame.

Someone is God who had a common name

That you might give a child or animal.

It happens overnight. The world is changed.

The bottles in the cellar all decant.

The stars sign the new cosmos at a slant.

And everybody's plans are rearranged.

Today we meet our maker, in a flash

That turns the ash of yesterday to flesh.

To the Green Man (2004)

To the Green Man

Lord of the returning leaves, of sleepers

Waking in their tunnels among roots,

Of heart and bush and fire-headed stag,

Of all things branching, stirring the blood like sap,

Pray for us in your small commemorations:

The facet of stained glass, the carved face

Lapped by decorations on the column side,

And the entry in the reference book that lists you

As forester, pub sign, keeper of golf courses.

King for a day, or week, then sacrificed,

Drunk on liquor made from honey, urged

To blossom at your leisure, and caressed—

The temptation is to think of you without envy.

In Fewston, Yorkshire, near the open moor,

You are set in a church window above the altar.

Wreathed and strangled, amber-glazed, you wear

A look of non-surprise, a victim's cunning,

Though your tongue hangs as dumb as any death.

Elsewhere, when you make your appearances,

Out of your mouth stems and oak leaves grow—

Like speech or silence? Your eyes are empty cups.

Pray, vestige-secret of the trees, for us,

Surprised and pleased to find you any place.

Testimony of a Roasted Chicken

Standing in drizzle in the twilit piazza,
Beside the lean Franciscan with his p.a. system,
One of the hilltown's aging bachelors,
Rumpled and plump and damp and pompadoured,
Tells the buzzing mike, the falling rain
And darkness, about Jesus, *la via, la verità, la vita.*
From lit-up bars, a few of us look out at him,
Knowing and pitying and finally indifferent.

How different, later in the bakery,
—Saturday night, buying Sunday's bread—
When he, the sad sack who lives with his mother,
Comes to pick up the meal cooked for him.
Smiling, *la fornaia* brings it out,
A capon fat as he is, trussed and steaming,
And casting over all an enchantment of rosemary,
Making every mouth a well of taste.
"*Che profumo, eh!*" says the baker, and she grins,
As he whose testimony we ignored
Receives his tasty supper from her hands
And steers it past our eyes into the night
To feast on by himself or with his mother,
While we, watching him go, wish we could have some.

Butterflies Under Persimmon

I heard a woman
    State once that because
He peered so closely

At a stream of ants
    On the damp, naked
Limb of a fruit tree,

She fell for her husband.
    She wanted to be studied
With that attention,

To fascinate as if
    She were another species,
Whose willingness to be

Looked at lovingly
    Was her defense, to be
Like a phenomenon

Among leaves, a body
    That would make him leave
His body in the act of loving,

Beautifully engrossed.

    I can't remember what
She looked like. I never met

The husband. But leaning close

    To the newly dropped
Persimmon in the wet grass,

And the huddle of four

    Or five hungry satyrs,
Drab at first glance, the dull

Brown of age spots, flitting

    Away in too many
Directions, too quickly

To count exactly, small

    As they are, in the shade
At the tree's base; leaning

Out of the sunlight, as if

I could take part in the feast there,
Where, mid-September,

The persimmons drop,
    So ripe and taut a touch
Can break the skin;

Leaning close enough
    To trouble the eye-spotted
Satyrs, no bigger than

Eyelids, and the fritillaries,
    Their calmer companions,
Like floating shreds of fire,

Whose feet have organs
    Of taste that make their tongues
Uncoil in reflex with

Goodness underfoot,
    I thought of that woman's
Lover, there on my belly

In sun and shadow,

And wished I could be like that.

Astragaloi

We know there must be consciousness in things,

    In bits of gravel pecked up by a hen

To grind inside her crop, and spider silk

    Just as it hardens stickily in air,

And even those things paralyzed in place,

    The wall brick, the hat peg, the steel beam

Inside the skyscraper, and lost, forgotten,

    And buried in ancient tombs, the toys and games.

Those starry jacks, those knucklebones of glass

    Meant for the dead to play with, toss and catch

Back of the hand and read the patterns of,

    Diversions to beguile the endless time,

Never to be picked up again . . . They're thinking,

    Surely, all of them. They are lost in thought.

Fox Night

What have I done to merit that regard?
Seeing the fox, I thought of diction like that:
Merit that regard, as if the wild demanded
A formal recognition of its grace
When passing through our world. What *had* I done,
So that I thought the world, at least my family,
Should know a fox was looking back at me?
V of head and ears tilted, lean waist
Humped with a serpent's frozen listening,
It poised like the green snake on the back road
My girls and I had found one summer day,
Back when we found such things on summer days.
The snake had let us study, then urge it on
To belly-waddle sideways, s- and elbowing,
Clumsy only because we made it hurry,
Into the roadside vetch and vinca blossoms.
It had endured us with the noble patience
Of relics, like an ancient copper bracelet
Uncoiled. And yet it flicked its tongue out, testing.
But with the fox, its red fur drenched in shadows,
Only the tail-tip gathering enough streetlight
To show its whipped-up, egg-white whiteness, I

Was by myself, come out to stow some trash,

The TV muttering in the den behind me.

The fox had come to eat the fall persimmons,

The harvest of the tree in our front yard,

Acknowledged me, and turned away, of course,

And crossed the road back through a screen of oaks,

A wall that halved the sky, with chinks of starlight.

There was no one to instruct, no one to show

That happiness, though speechless, could be shared.

And so I made a comment to myself

In language that, if I'd repeated it,

Might have made my daughters look at one another

And wonder at the nature of the world.

As Close as Breathing

Called or not called, God is present.
Delphic Oracle

The flicker doesn't know his call's not needed,

But he's not calling God. He lifts his beak

To show his black bib, as the females chuckle

Off in the oaks somewhere. They hear him all right.

The metal gutters make a fine percussion.

If God is present, why then aren't we talking?

The sugar water feeder stews in the sunshine.

The mud daubers fall asleep there, suckling.

The hummingbirds blur past. Last summer

One came with a ruby wart on her neck,

An imperfection that was almost perfect.

Does God assume our silence is a call?

If I write down the day I see the first swift

(Never the same day but always April),

It's not a prayer, though it may count as one.

They like grade schools where one cold chimney stands,

An obelisk in a cloud of darting hieroglyphs.

∞

Words too can be as close to us as breathing.

A spider's dragline, glinting like a thought,

Trolls through depths of shade and morning light.

The hemlock limbs bob as if at anchor.

And a pair of downy woodpeckers swoops up

To the seed bell at my study window. Everything answers.

Everything says back, "I am present, too."

In the Tube

They beat the edge
    Of the dawn light,
        The pearly pre-glow

Right at their heels,
    The three boys
        Carrying the fourth

Rolled in a sheet.
    They all had taken
        Something the night

Before in a beach
    House and this one
        Drowned in his sleep.

They acted quickly,
    These instinctive
        Athletes who cross

The faces of tons
    Of crushing water
        Which refrain

From curling over

  And burying them

    Alive because they

Are nimble, quick,

  Tuned to the wit

    Of their survivors'

Bodies. They hurried

  From the running car

    And laid their friend

Like a Sunday paper

  On his parents' doorstep,

    And drove off to

The place where the sharp

  New light would score

    The wave crests and they

Would ride below them,

  Dodging the onrush.

In Church with Hart Crane

This white Doubleday Anchor book

With the fuchsia pink M of the Brooklyn Bridge on the cover

Was my prayerbook in a church without prayerbooks.

I sat in the back shadows, knowing God could see

And so could my father speaking in the pulpit.

And I read, "It was a kind and northern face"

And liked that one and liked "Repose of Rivers"

Even more, as the singing river lost itself,

Hearing "wind flaking sapphire," in the sea

"Beyond the dykes." There was a sea beyond

The holy space behind my father's back,

Beyond the baptistry that cupped its portion,

Unsalty, tepid, blessed to rinse off sin.

A block away the Pacific swarmed with its rivers

And the wind really did flake Sapphire,

And Emerald, and Ruby—names of streets.

And in my hands the white book hummed.

There was poetry equal to its voices

In the drab hymnal slotted in the pew

And in my father's sinuous braid of sentences.

But I wouldn't know that for years. He wanted me

To be good. I wanted to write a poem as good

As "Repose of Rivers," as "My Grandmother's
Love Letters," as "Black Tambourine," the three
I thought I understood.

                       How many awful times
I've sat in church since then, believing
That I was neither good nor good enough
To write the poems I thought I understood.
With Christ invisible on his bloodless cross,
With Crane dissolved in the spindrift a block away,
I read in church, and couldn't imagine either one
Seated beside me in his fishy clothes,
Putting a salty finger on the page, saying,
"Read this one again. You haven't gotten it."
The most important person in the room,
Among the visible, was robed and large
And knew what I was doing, reading poetry,
And didn't say a word. I would remember.
I *have* remembered, and in my classrooms ignore
The sleeping boys and girls and the waking dreamers
Turning toward the window like sunflowers,
While some conspiring phantom, like Hart or Jesus,
Drifts past, beckoning.

The book still falls open to those poems,

The ones I bowed my head to as if in prayer,

Asking to be a river, a love letter, a black tambourine.

George Herbert

Who is wise enough today to be George Herbert,

    Who though he lost his temper could remain

Tractable to a loving, patient voice?

    Washing his parishioners' feet, as the collar chafed

And softened. Writing his fastidious verses,

    Like the coffin-shaped stones of his century,

Decked with skulls and propped in churchyard corners.

    Death, a puddle of dust, drew under his door,

Like talcum powder, clinging to his shoes.

    And love, whose board he hammered with his fist,

Drew him in and offered him its meat,

    That ambiguous unambiguous word. George Herbert

Was wise enough to sit and clean his plate.

The Excitement

My grandfather was given to believing
In ghosts beside the Holy Ghost. As a boy
He felt an invisible hand clap on his head
As a voice murmured, "You are in my power."
As a man he heard his mother's voice in the pulpit.
In some lights he could picture people's souls
As shrouds of fog or stray bits of apparel,
Shirt tails poking out, secret banners waving.
He knew what faith could do, that hidden star
Imploded at the galaxy's black heart,
And he had faith. He wanted a technique.
He knew there was a way to make his faith
Devour its cosmic doubts and spit them back
As the moving mountains of both space and time.
Time led him on to death. And space confined him.
He thought—if he could only pull them apart
And not unweave himself. He believed his soul
Was safe, because it also hid within him,
Separate and pristine, a bead of meaning,
A seed in time and space which, once beyond them,
Would blossom in eternity, just waiting.
But let him move this saltshaker across the table.

If he could do that, simply with a thought,

What couldn't he do? What my grandfather wanted

Was mind enough to move things with a thought.

And he believed that faith was a technique,

But there had to be others. Jesus came

To tell him there were no others, and faith itself

Was not invented to move saltshakers.

But Jesus came to him. Who wouldn't want that?

Who wouldn't want to walk with him in a garden,

On a sunny day, in a cloister of fresh flowers?

He would make you feel special and would not flatter,

But speak about the world that you could make,

You would have the power to make, which he would give you.

No one could get enough of such a person.

Charisma (the heroin of personality)—

My grandfather wanted to have that, too:

To be the one the young monks flocked behind,

Quacking their questions, and to stop every so often

To answer them like a cloud across the sun—

Not ominous but with refreshing coolness.

Gandhi, it is said, took walks like that.

One entered in the flow of his current interests,

In honey bees, or salt recovery, or spinning wheels.

Who wouldn't want in the cool of the day to walk

With one who knew everything about you,

More even than you knew? That was the secret.

The faith that walked on water was a power

My grandfather wanted, with its homely gifts

For treating time and space like salt and pepper.

A dash of either and the real was changed

Into the spicy soup of the unreal.

To taste that, and to make that simply happen.

And doesn't it matter to want something better

And not a raise or more job self-esteem,

But something on a plane so rarefied

You lived there like a migrant hummingbird

Or Monarch butterfly, crossing the Gulf,

Going north or south and feeding on the sugar

Of ecstasy, existing in that wingbeat,

The sky, the expanse of water, no land in sight?

To put his hand through air into the future,

And heal the dying child. To reach back with ten fingers

And raise the loved one, waiting in the grave.

Because he knew that Christ had done these things,

My grandfather wanted to do them, too.

He wanted to leave his mark on the eternal,

To manipulate the supernatural stuff

That he was sure was everywhere, like the airwaves.

And on the radio he threw his voice

Against the willing air that rippled with it.

He called himself the Shepherd of the Air

And gathered his flock of insubstantial strays

From the antennas of Los Angeles.

I've told you this so you can know this man,

My grandfather, a little, as I tell my story,

The only real ghost story I know,

A holy ghost story, complete with blood and terror,

For it unfolds at night, and someone or something

Risen from the dead plays a crucial role

At scaring the living Jesus out of somebody.

It may be Jesus himself who did the scaring.

It was a dry and cool November evening.

Los Angeles collected all its lights,

Some still, some strung on moving threads,

Into its basin beside the ocean's darkness.

This was the vastness where my grandfather worked,

Alone in his church office, recording a sermon

On tape, and playing it back, and hearing himself

Explain the spiritual power of some new thing,

Some drug or diet or mental exercise

That had excited him. The ghost was coming,

The first he'd ever seen, after years of wishing

That he could see them everywhere.

Hypnotist, Metaphysician, Parapsychologist,

Quester in the Dreamworld, Channeler,

These were roles he played or he pretended.

And now a real ghost, torn from the cosmos,

Was coming to his office to address him.

There was a step, ringing on the stairwell,

Although my grandfather couldn't hear it,

Or hear the doorknob turn, the presence enter,

For he was listening to himself quote scripture,

"Behold, I stand at the door and knock." Red letters

His voice turned into living words, like song.

Then, out of the tangled mesh of chapter and verse,

The blood of Jesus' speech on the filmy page

Spilled suddenly across the carpeted floor.

My grandfather looked up and saw the man,

And not as in his Bible recitations.

Bleeding, yes, but dressed in business clothes.

In fact, dressed as he was in business clothes,

About my grandfather's height, about his size,

Bald with a little silver hair combed sideways,

And wearing horn-rimmed glasses, lips parted

To speak. The ghost had on the same white shirt.

And both wore ties, the same tie, with the same knot.

But Grandfather couldn't see these things for the blood,

The blood coming from the hands and feet—

Bare feet in a business suit, with familiar hands,

And the blood from the famous wounds printing the carpet

And spreading over the things on the glass-topped desk.

The bleeding man in the dark suit looked familiar.

And his voice, too, sounded strange in the same way

Grandfather's voice did when he played it back.

But the question that he asked as he stood there bleeding

Was not one Grandfather ever asked himself:

"Why are you wasting your time on all this nonsense?"

He saw a soul wounded by his existence
And told the world and us it was Jesus Christ.

The years into old age and death were set then.
And I have often thought about those years.
For this was the peak moment in family history,
The Lord come unto Granddad to rebuke him
And all the supernatural confirmed.
For he did not turn away from his desires,
But took a new way, or an old way he'd forgotten.
Life with the Holy Spirit, as he called it,
Led him to crowds as he had never known them,
The leaning forward masses who could see
Something peculiar that they wanted, too,
Bathing the old man in its thrilling spotlight.
Even as his body gave up its powers—
Abandoning a right hand's cunning, breaking a hip,
And draining from the corner of his mouth—
Wheeled into the presence of believers,
He basked in their true love and stuck by his story.
They led him a merry dance until he died.

Five Psalms

1.

Let us think of God as a lover
    Who never calls,
Whose pleasure in us is aroused
    In unrepeatable ways,
God as a body we cannot
    Separate from desire,
Saying to us, "Your love
    Is only physical."
Let us think of God as a bronze
    With green skin
Or a plane that draws the eye close
    To the texture of paint.
Let us think of God as life,
    A bacillus or virus,
As death, an igneous rock
    In a quartz garden.
Then, let us think of kissing
    God with the kisses
Of our mouths, of lying with God,
    As sea worms lie,
Snugly petrifying
    In their coral shirts.

Let us think of ourselves
        As part of God,
Neither alive nor dead,
        But like Alpha, Omega,
Glyphs and hieroglyphs,
        Numbers, data.

2.
First forgive the silence
        That answers prayer,
Then forgive the prayer
        That stains the silence.

Excuse the absence
        That feels like presence,
Then excuse the feeling
        That insists on presence.

Pardon the delay
        Of revelation,
Then ask pardon for revealing
        Your impatience.

∞

Forgive God

    For being only a word,

Then ask God to forgive

    The betrayal of language.

3.

God of the Syllable

    God of the Word

God Who Speaks to Us

    God Who Is Dumb

The One God The Many

    God the Unnameable

God of the Human Face

    God of the Mask

God of the Gene Pool

    Microbe Mineral

God of the Sparrow's Fall

    God of the Spark

God of the Act of God

    Blameless Jealous

God of Surprises
    And Startling Joy

God Who Is Absent
    God Who Is Present
God Who Finds Us
    In Our Hiding Places

God Whom We Thank
    Whom We Forget to Thank
Father God   Mother
    Inhuman Infant

Cosmic Chthonic
    God of the Nucleus
Dead God   Living God
    Alpha God   Zed

God Whom We Name
    God Whom We Cannot Name
When We Open Our Mouths
    With the Name God   Word God

∞

4.

The new day cancels dread
    And dawn forgives all sins,
All the judgments of insomnia,
    As if they were only dreams.

The ugly confrontation
    After midnight, with the mirror,
Turns white around the edges
    And burns away like frost.

Daylight undoes gravity
    And lightness responds to the light.
The new day lifts all weight,
    Like stepping off into space.

Where is that room you woke to,
    By clock-light, at 3 a.m.?
Nightmare's many mansions,
    Falling, have taken it with them.

∞

The new day, the day's newness,

    And the wretchedness that, you thought,

Would never, never depart,

    Meet—and there is goodbye.

A bad night lies ahead

    And a new day beyond that—

A simple sequence, but hard

    To remember in the right order.

5.

Lord of dimensions and the dimensionless,

Wave and particle, all and none,

Who lets us measure the wounded atom,

Who lets us doubt all measurement,

When in this world we betray you

Let us be faithful in another.

Canticle

Beautiful repetition, the caress repeated, again,
That makes one say and repeat, "Don't stop."

Reiteration, restatement, the beat brushed into skin;
The pulse responding to breath, counted, touched.

Beautiful pattern of change, cyclical as blood,
The axle pivots, the planet wanders.

The moon comes back and leaves, a total story or slice
Of life, shining with meaning, like a life.

Beautiful repetition, the haze of new grass
Rises from scattered seeds, a green dawn.

A chickadee's claim rings the seed ball by the window.
The world tilts, too, a bell dented by song.

Look at it happen again, always in a new pattern:
Famine again, war, after the odd peace.

Habit, the great deadener, narrows our affections
To one face, reappearing in the mirror.

∞

Look at it happen again, always for the first time:
Death of the father, the mother, absolute.

No way to bring them back, except to become them.
Tragic re-enactment, beautiful repetition.

Song of Roland

Roland was a Paladin of Charlemagne,
And he was my mother's cousin. The Paladin
Served Charlemagne and died, blowing his horn.
The cousin spent a day with her at the fair
Over sixty years ago. The great Paladin
Enjoys an epic named after him.
The cousin is remembered as a big kid
Who never grew up. His first wife left him,
Taking only the pillows from the pool furniture.
Roland the epic hero was betrayed
By a fellow Paladin. Roland the cousin bought
A box of face powder for his younger cousin,
And on the octopus, which they had ridden
So often the owner let them ride for free,
He convinced her to open up the box.
Roland's horn resounds through ages
Of high school lit classes. There's a cloud
The carnie thinks is an explosion and stops
His ride, and banishes the powdered laughing children,
Roland, the young hero, and my mother
Creamy with dust in a new blue coat.
Roland's song comes down from the Pyrenees.

His namesake went back to school, after his wife left,

Became a mining engineer, worked in North Dakota,

Married again, learned after the death of his parents

He'd been adopted, was devastated, and died

In his late 30's of congenital heart failure. He lives on, though.

An old woman remembers that day at the fair

And as much of his life and fate as any of us

Is likely to have immortalized in song.

Over the River and Through the Woods

Back streets, byways, eroded, gouged, patched wide spots

Between chain link and cinderblock,

Lanes too pretty a word, alleys too much glamour,

Channels of gravel, asphalt scar tissue, mud and gray dust,

Passages past doors without handles and empty parking lots

Where the leanest wine-dark vagrant

Hikes his pants up over his non-hips after pissing,

Or less than that, regions where no one does anything

Except pass through, shortcuts to lead garbage trucks to dumpsters,

Delivery trucks to loading docks, drunks to a place to sleep,

Charmless, rough, pitted and potholed,

Leafless, except for overlapping leaves of tar,

The last to be served and absolutely necessary,

Where milky coffee puddles turn to cracked frosting

And a wasp or butterfly (a cabbage white) wets its tongue,

Part of the radiant, hidden world, part of what makes it

Radiant, hidden, the world,

Places to baptize a sudden yen for new life,

On the way to grandmother's house.

The Secret Ocean

When you were little girls, I brought you here
    To light weaving on water among trees,
With one of you beside me, walking along,

    The other on my shoulders, talking to herself.
We found this place beside a baseball field
    In a flood plain, flooded with meadowlarks.

And on a jut of fossil-bearing limestone
    We pitched our half-hour camp. Strewn on rock
Were shells that had been eaten out that morning,

    Empty debris of crayfish, turbinate snails.
The torrent raveled past, a golden craftwork,
    No deeper than reflection. A speckled dancing

Took place upon the wavelets and the air,
    A water strider sort of dance, a shifting
Greened by the leaves like lenses overhead.

    I think I named it after one of you,
Claire's Secret Ocean, Zoë's Secret Sea,
    Far from the actual oceans you'd not seen yet.

Under the cottonwoods, among acacia stalks,

    We watched the nimble acts of light and shadow,

The harmless tumult, the dimpled water tension.

    Neither of you knew that we were there

To calm and change the color of my thought,

    To ease its glaring pressure for a moment.

And we have been together other places

    For the same reason, which I can now reveal—

There have been times I thought my head would crack,

    Only to have you both demand ice cream.

It's been a long time since we've walked together

    For reasons you didn't have to understand.

If you were younger I wouldn't be less fearful,

    Now that the monster shadowing you is not

The wounded ego of your harmless father,

    But something that would harm you if it could

And in old fashioned terms has had its way

      With all of us. I think of the first, stunned day

Outside of Eden, going through the motions—

      No—learning motions no one had yet dreamed of.

And menace, like a new electric nimbus,

      Surrounding everything, invisibly.

And no one to walk with us but each other.

      And yet it could be that these private walks

To places like the secret ocean, trailing

      Beside a darkened, mute, distracted parent,

Were preparations for new valleys of the shadow,

      Fearing no evil, because someone was with you.

Summer

At the end of a bad year, the swifts
Offer their bodies to the air we breathe,
Saying, "This is the real world," as she did,
Turning to me on the bed. "This is
The real world."

And on the eve of another
Uncertainty, the fireflies cover their lamps.
Their blazing codes, sinking with us
To sleep, echo, "This is the real world. This
Is the real world."

And as the dogwoods
Forfeit their beauty, and August ignites
Its first leaf, there is consolation
In knowing that this is the real
World.

For she was naked. And I believed her.

Coyotes

Is this world truly fallen? They say no.

For there's the new moon, there's the Milky Way,

There's the rattler with a wren's egg in its mouth,

And there's the panting rabbit they will eat.

They sing their wild hymn on the dark slope,

Reading the stars like notes of hilarious music.

Is this a fallen world? How could it be?

And yet we're crying over the stars again

And over the uncertainty of death,

Which we suspect will divide us all forever.

I'm tired of those who broadcast their certainties,

Constantly on their cellphones to their redeemer.

Is this a fallen world? For them it is.

But there's that starlit burst of animal laughter.

The day has sent its fires scattering.

The night has risen from its burning bed.

Our tears are proof that love is meant for life

And for the living. And this chorus of praise,

Which the pet dogs of the neighborhood are answering

Nostalgically, invites our answer, too.

Is this a fallen world? How could it be?

A Pair of Tanagers

The scarlet male, his green mate, their black wings
Beside the A/C unit in the dull dirt:

They look at first like a child's abandoned toys.
But ants and iridescent flies have found them,

Working along the seams of the shut beaks
And the dark indentations of the eyelids.

You want to give something like this a moral:
Like, the woods these days are full of hard illusions,

Or, never fly north if you think you're flying south,
Or, stay above rooftops; if you meet yourself

Coming, it's too late; death is a big surprise.
And their death together certainly startles us.

Stopped short. But how recently in the rain forest,
How recently in the place they were first named,

Reflected on the Amazon, the Orinoco,
Headlong from Brazil, into our window.

❦

You want to give something like this a moral

Or see it as an omen, as a portent.

And then, the long journeying comes to mind,

Together such a distance, to this end.

Prayer for Our Daughters

May they never be lonely at parties
Or wait for mail from people they haven't written
Or still in middle age ask God for favors
Or forbid their children things they were never forbidden.

May hatred be like a habit they never developed
And can't see the point of, like gambling or heavy drinking.
If they forget themselves, may it be in music
Or the kind of prayer that makes a garden of thinking.

May they enter the coming century
Like swans under a bridge into enchantment
And take with them enough of this century
To assure their grandchildren it really happened.

May they find a place to love, without nostalgia
For some place else that they can never go back to.
And may they find themselves, as we have found them,
Complete at each stage of their lives, each part they add to.

May they be themselves, long after we've stopped watching.
May they return from every kind of suffering

(Except the last, which doesn't bear repeating)

And be themselves again, both blessed and blessing.

Epistles (2007)

In the Clouds

Simply by thinking I stood among the clouds. They surrounded and passed me, being and becoming. Blood released into clear water. Breath into cold air. Formlessness entering form, forced into form. Breathing felt huge then smaller than a cell. And I thought, "Don't the clouds themselves feel ambivalent between heaven and earth, hardly more substantial than their shadows? They come into being as randomly as we do. And they disintegrate. They go. What is the lifespan of a cloud? We want to float among them, loving the colossal, shot through with crooked pins of fire, towering side by side."

How did I get up there? I was thinking about changing my life and wanted to talk to a cloud, since clouds are always changing. And the clouds said, "How long has it been since you felt completely happy? Because you are always dissatisfied, always disappointed—it has been a long time. Talk to us. We are admired and disparaged. We are less than everything you compare us to except nothingness. We are not nothing. Talk to us. Our silence, like the new shapes we are forever assuming, will be sympathetic. In the clouds, you will understand yearning as you never have and come back to earth changed, who knows how? Surrender your skin, your bones. But we will not hold you up. We are as ineffectual as cattle, turning steep white faces beside the road, to watch you spin out of control. Placid as the love of God. Fall out of the sky, go sliding down the icy face of the air, we will watch, a little lightning might flicker in a distant bulb of fiber glass. Come to us as the exhalation of your speech, the spirit trapped inside your webs of flesh torn free. We are the embodiment of detachment. You know us best when we are most distant and you are least afraid, when we are most moving and you are unmoved."

Brothers and sisters, consider the taste of cloud in a Sherpa's mouth, of fog in a surfer's throat. Consider the flocculent muscle of the cumulus. The icy elevation of the cirrus. But especially the thunderhead, full of zeal, hurrying in with its bevelled wind, white slanting rain, its electric personality, its aftermath. Consider how the clouds predict one another and how they break up, pulling a new body behind them. The farmer's wide open perspective. The office worker's sidelong glimpse. Weeks of drab overcast. A single afternoon of separate sailwhite drifters. Clouds flat and dull as lampblack, clouds with the contours of the brain, clouds like sheets of paper. I have read that even in an empty sky there exists water vapor enough to make a cloud. Belief enough to make a God.

As they change, clouds grow neither better nor worse. They alter because it is their nature to alter. They can fill us with joy or cast a stagnant sorrow over our days. Such is life under the clouds. In the clouds it is different. But if we live in the clouds, we have to take the earth with us.

For the Birds

When you wake up, raising the film over your eyes, in a hollow of
boughs or bark, you are always hungry. And you all talk at once. Each
twig has an opinion and holds a singing fabric sewn with discussions
of lice, offspring, height above ground, eyesight, mates, one-night
stands, best routes to Canada once the warm weather comes, the
taste of this bug, that bug, spittle needed to mat human hair, mud's
pliancy, the housework of the sky. We think that none of you has an
insight into the afterlife. But you all remember birth and the cramped
translucent dark before the break-out.

I am bored. I need birds. Not flight but activity, not serene detachment
sailing but intense engagement hunting. Look me in the eyes, frontal,
head on. And I admire you. Study me askance. And I adore you. Even the
moa in the museum case. The trinket hanging from the Christmas tree.

Incurious witnesses, feathers dabbled in blood, poking your noses
in the wounded hands and feet. What did St. Francis tell you? Be
yourselves, little ones, and you will praise God.

For how many of us were you the first word?

Trouble sleeping, I think of you in the netted aviary. There among reaching fronds and green blades, you hovered at my sister's washed floating hair, patient to take a single sand-colored strand that, buoyed by static, reached out half-limp to be taken. She felt it go with a little cry when the root broke from its anchor of scalp-skin.

And this morning, there's an oil smear on the sliding glass door to the patio, and in it, dangling gray breast feathers—five of them, like milkweed fluff. One of you caromed off the hard sky and left this pattern, as precise as fish scales, scalloped on the glass like a record in rock. Veronica's napkin. The Shroud of Turin.

Woodpeckers, hairy or downy. Red-bellied. Pileated. Flickers. Cardinals. Brown thrashers. A single rose-breasted grosbeak. Once, a tumbling flock of drunken cedar waxwings, chirping like crickets. Red-tailed hawks with breasts like lampshades. Great horned owls conversing at dawn, in January. Screech owls in their red phases. Mockingbirds copying mockingbirds. Chimney swifts back from Peru to the same elementary school chimney. Kingbirds on powerlines. Bluebirds in pairs. Blue jays in gangs. To be a man who surrounds his house with birds. To be a woman visited by wings. To say to the turkey vulture overhead, "Sister." To say, "Brother," to the starling in the swirling flock.

∞

If your call and response first thing in the morning make us hold hands and smile in the dark, as we lie in bed, it's because we're not alone in the world. And when letters like this one are written, it is because we are.

To the Trees

How do you feel as you rear up or hunch over to seek sunlight? When young, as pliant almost as water, when old, second only to rock. I think you must feel that roots are better than roads, that the avenue to the sky is best straight up or crookedly up. That whatever happens around you is no more than rain or snow, even the building that embraces you, even the saw and stump remover that eat up all trace of you.

For the present you are stone, but let the wind rise and you sing and dance like bamboo. Your children are the dapples of sunshine in shade. Your ancestors bask on the mossy facets of your bark. And within is a coming and going of thirst and records of thirst, of flesh that fire would love to taste. You know the math that sends the fire branching upward. You know the myth that lights the candelabra. Planets and stars gleam on your smallest twig ends.

You have held back the body of the wind. You have held back the onslaught of the heat. You have given me the idea of depth. You have revealed the nesting of microcosms, all while staying in one place. We came down from you and stood upright like you. Because you will not rush along with us we cut you down.

∞

It's what's inside and outside that counts. Hollow with ant meal, your blossoms and leaves still come. Solid as granite, you can stand deadgray for decades. You bleed, you break, you rot. The massive inner framework fades, and there's a limp limb, a branch of brown leaves among green, a bridge across a stream, a back-breaking fall on a ranch-style house. You rot, you break, you bleed. You go up in smoke, sideways in fire, down and down and down.

In my metamorphosis, she appears in the doorway, wet from the shower and looking for a towel. We catch each other by surprise, goddess and little boy, and we are both changed. At times she is a row of eucalyptus, where the trees and the sunlight between them are the same smooth color. It is my fate to hunt for her everywhere except where that tree grows. At times I am pyracantha under her windowsill, burning to speak. It is her fate to believe I have nothing to say.

You are life to those who hold fast to you, but standing apart on the lawn, don't you all long for the forest canopy? To join and blot out the sky, with a dancing floor lifted to the sun for hawks and monkeys and orchids in the higher parts of shadow? Don't you all long to rise up and erect your shade?

∞

Let me be neither branch nor leaf but one facet of your bark, deeply incised on all sides, gray in dry sunny weather, and in rain, showing a face of turquoise.

On the Street

He jogs in, a V of sweat on his t-shirt. He strides in, pushing a baby carriage. Wearing a Walkman, he saunters in. He barrels in in his truck, and stops, and gets out. He tells the taxi driver to let him off here. He thanks the person who gave him a lift, opens the car door, and invites her to stay. Brakes his bicycle at the brush heap in the cul de sac, dismounts, and starts calling our names. Our first names. Appears one day, like the blossoms on the redbud, and captures our attention. We know it's spring, and we know him.

What's the word on the street? The word is made flesh on the street. The word is made person, place, and thing. The word is steel, concrete, fibre-optic cable, ceramic and saliva, aluminum and blood, axle grease and fingernails, hair and glass. It is the leaf of the sidewalk weed and the soft desiring soul inside the truck cab. It is the footprint tracked a little ways beyond the puddle and the foot still thinking of where it stepped. Anonymous and public, the word is that if you're good, you'll be happy, if you're happy, you'll be good. Suffer and remain private. Receive aid, and see your savior on the news. Out the door, into the blaring, shining welcome, from which there is no escape, the word on the street is lord. Tang of diesel fumes, fellow fragrance of men and women, music of the spheres of influence burning to illuminate the word, the word in every molecule that starts a sense, these—and that face that passes and travels with you a little way beyond the sight of it. They are the word on the street. And the word is knowledge like a cellphone ringing with all the others.

Inside, behind the showroom window, two men in shirtsleeves and ties and a woman in her power suit watched. One held a telephone. Outside we passed the group beginning to assemble around the lady who lay on her right cheek. She wore a felt hat and a cloth coat, both a grayer version of her blue eye, her left eye which stared at our feet. The right side of her face—cheek, eye, half her mouth—was pressed hard against the sidewalk. The half of her mouth we could see showed, in its grin, an effort to do or say—no one knew. Her eye, watching our feet, was painted marble, showing outer and inner knowledge, straining to know more. As if she were studying the street itself—the pavement where we were passing and our feet—studying for a clue to why she had fallen there, why she walked there, lived there, put on her old lady's attire on an early spring day, and went out, to do errands, and found her way to this vigil, this post.

What was she looking at? At the grain of the cement she felt under her cheek and its color. At the rims of shoe soles that stopped and those that pivoted and moved on. The soles made a grainy scraping that her hidden ear caught and she was looking at the source of that sound. There is too much on the street. All you can do is know the smallest portion. May it save her.

Through the Waves

If I spoke to you through the waves, which one would catch your
attention, the ripple that wet your knee or the beach-pounder shaking
your bed? If I spoke to you through the waves, would you remember
what I said as a series of glittering, nostalgic video images, far from
the ocean, each as harmless as cotton floss?

Small, gray, glassy, like a pleasant hour reading, transparent to
its heart of jellyfish and seaweed. Large, swift, green, opaque and
grinning whitely, asking for a quick response. Unanswerable, coming
down startled, all bulk and foam, which you must dive under. Each
bearing a message. Lovely swelling blue, giving you time to move
into position, just as it peaks and you feel its force behind you.
Black, making her arms glisten as she swims at night, belly and face
like candles of phosphorus. Colorless, dismal rippling, coming to
shore over shingle, cold enough to turn fingernails purple. And the
warm giant that beckons before it sweeps you under to toil among
churning roots.

If I spoke to you through the waves, would you see your face reflected
in the upthrust wall of words? If I spoke to you through the waves,
would your revery before their arrival ever turn into understanding?

∞

To quiet myself I used to remember being lifted and carried by them, buoyed as they broke around me, and standing up in the shallows among the frothy rubble of their collapse, then wading back out, swimming out to meet them as they continued coming to shore. That would help me to fall asleep when I first began to live apart from them. As years passed, and I moved deeper inland, I would dream of them. In one recurring dream I walked along a sea wall and they broke against it, and I saw in their explosions, they were made of pigeon feathers or anthracite or my parents' faces or red oak leaves. Though enormous they broke slowly and benignly, their spray drifting like confetti and dissolving in air. But once I began to dream of them I no longer tried to remember them when I couldn't sleep: to do so only made me more wakeful. A time came when I no longer dreamt of them and they ceased altogether to have any reality for me. They had been lifted and shaped by homesickness. They had emerged composed of dreamstuff for reasons I could never fathom. Now they are a single idea: the image of body and soul together as one.

If I spoke to you through the waves, would you see that I mean more than the moon and less, more than the wind and less, more than the sea floor and less, more than more, less than less? If I spoke to you through the waves, how many times would I have to repeat myself?

Out of chaos, beyond theory, into a life that peaks and breaks, the wave emerges. The shore where it dies lies ahead and waits, unseen. A life must peak as it rides up the shallow approach, steepen, and break. I want you to think of yourself like that, of your body and soul like that, one flesh traveling to shore, to collapse, all that way to end by darkening the sand and evaporating. Where do you go? You repeat in other waves, repeat and repeat. Each bears a message. Each has a meaning.

If I spoke to you through the waves, I would continue to bring them to life until, looking at how they laid themselves at your feet, at how even the greatest ended as film on sand, you said, "Someone is trying to tell me something." And I would not stop.

Jonathan Rodgers

MARK JARMAN is the author of nine books of poetry: *North Sea* (1978), *The Rote Walker* (1981), *Far and Away* (1985), *The Black Riviera* (1990), *Iris* (1992), *Questions for Ecclesiastes* (1997), *Unholy Sonnets* (2000), *To the Green Man* (2004), and *Epistles* (2007). He has also published two collections of his prose, *The Secret of Poetry* (2000) and *Body and Soul: Essays on Poetry* (2001). Jarman is an elector of the American Poets' Corner at the Cathedral Church of Saint John the Divine in New York City. His awards include a Joseph Henry Jackson Award for his poetry, grants from the National Endowment for the Arts in poetry, and a John Simon Guggenheim Memorial Foundation fellowship in poetry. His book *The Black Riviera* won the 1991 Poets' Prize. *Questions for Ecclesiastes* won the 1998 Lenore Marshall Poetry prize from the Academy of American Poets and *The Nation* magazine. He is Centennial Professor of English at Vanderbilt University.